KU-406-305

FRENCH
COOKERY

Previous page, left to right Assorted cheeses; Ham and Parsley Mould (page 29); Veal Chops Dijonnaise (page 54); Leek Gratin (page 85); Chocolate Truffles (page 109).

Overleaf Cheese Soufflé (page 66).

Anne Willan

FRENCH COOKERY

Hamlyn

London · New York · Sydney · Toronto

Originally published under the title
Basic French Cookery
by H.P. Books, P.O. Box 5367, Tucson, AZ 85703

This edition published in 1983 by
The Hamlyn Publishing Group Limited
London · New York · Sydney · Toronto
Astronaut House, Feltham, Middlesex, England

© Anne Willan 1980

All rights reserved. No part of this publication may be reproduced, stored in a retrieval system, or transmitted, in any form or by any means, electronic, mechanical, photocopying, recording or otherwise, without the permission of The Hamlyn Publishing Group Limited

ISBN 0 600 32324 2

Cover photograph by Martin Brigdale
Illustrations by the Hayward Art Group

Filmset in 11 on 12pt Monophoto Garamond by
Servis Filmsetting Limited, Manchester
Printed in Denmark

Contents

Useful Facts and Figures

Notes on metrication

In this book quantities are given in metric and Imperial measures. Exact conversion from Imperial to metric measures does not usually give very convenient working quantities and so the metric measures have been rounded off into units of 25 grams. The table below shows the recommended equivalents.

Ounces	*Approx g to nearest whole figure*	*Recommended conversion nearest unit of 25*
1	28	25
2	57	50
3	85	75
4	113	100
5	142	150
6	170	175
7	198	200
8	227	225
9	255	250
10	283	275
11	312	300
12	340	350
13	368	375
14	396	400
15	425	425
16 (1 lb)	454	450
17	482	475
18	510	500
19	539	550
20 (1¼ lb)	567	575

Note: When converting quantities over 20 oz first add the appropriate figures in the centre column, then adjust to the nearest unit of 25. As a general guide, 1 kg (1000 g) equals 2.2 lb or about 2 lb 3 oz. This method of conversion gives good results in nearly all cases, although in certain pastry and cake recipes a more accurate conversion is necessary to produce a balanced recipe.

Liquid measures The millilitre has been used in this book and the following table gives a few examples.

Imperial	*Approx ml to nearest whole figure*	*Recommended ml*
¼ pint	142	150 ml
½ pint	283	300 ml
¾ pint	425	450 ml
1 pint	567	600 ml
1½ pints	851	900 ml
1¾ pints	992	1000 ml (1 litre)

Spoon measures All spoon measures given in this book are level unless otherwise stated.

Can sizes At present, cans are marked with the exact (usually to the nearest whole number) metric equivalent of the Imperial weight of the contents, so we have followed this practice when giving can sizes.

Oven temperatures

The table below gives recommended equivalents.

	°C	*°F*	*Gas Mark*
Very cool	110	225	¼
	120	250	½
Cool	140	275	1
	150	300	2
Moderate	160	325	3
	180	350	4
Moderately hot	190	375	5
	200	400	6
Hot	220	425	7
	230	450	8
Very hot	240	475	9

Notes for American and Australian users

In America the 8-oz measuring cup is used. In Australia metric measures are now used in conjunction with the standard 250-ml measuring cup. The Imperial pint, used in Britain and Australia, is 20 fl oz, while the American pint is 16 fl oz. It is important to remember that the Australian tablespoon differs from both the British and American tablespoons; the table below gives a comparison. The British standard tablespoon, which has been used throughout this book, holds 17.7 ml, the American 14.2 ml, and the Australian 20 ml. A teaspoon holds approximately 5 ml in all three countries.

British	*American*	*Australian*
1 teaspoon	1 teaspoon	1 teaspoon
1 tablespoon	1 tablespoon	1 tablespoon
2 tablespoons	3 tablespoons	2 tablespoons
3½ tablespoons	4 tablespoons	3 tablespoons
4 tablespoons	5 tablespoons	3½ tablespoons

An Imperial/American guide to solid and liquid measures.

Imperial	*American*
Solid measure	
1 lb butter or margarine	2 cups
1 lb flour	4 cups
1 lb granulated or castor sugar	2 cups
1 lb icing sugar	3 cups
8 oz rice	1 cup
Liquid measures	
¼ pint liquid	⅔ cup liquid
½ pint	1¼ cups
¾ pint	2 cups
1 pint	2½ cups
1½ pints	3¾ cups
2 pints	5 cups (2½ pints)

NOTE: When making any of the recipes in this book, only follow one set of measures as they are not interchangeable.

Introduction

The Techniques of French Cooking

Sauces

How to make a sauce of coating consistency Judging the correct consistency for a sauce is really a matter of experience. Coating consistency is the desired thickness of sauce that is neither gluey nor runny but adheres lightly to food. If it is too thick a sauce will taste unpleasant; if too thin, it will run off the food without coating it. One test is to dip a spoon into the sauce, lift it out and hold it rounded side up. If the sauce just clings to the spoon it is of light coating consistency and is the right consistency for sauces that will be served separately from the rest of the dish. For a thicker sauce to coat food, draw a finger across the back of the spoon – it should leave a clear trail.

How to prevent a skin forming When flour-based mixtures such as white and velouté sauces, choux pastry and soufflé mixtures are prepared in advance a skin may form on top. To prevent this, as soon as the mixture is cooked, rub the surface with butter to seal it from the air. Take a small piece of cold butter on a fork and dab it quickly over the surface of the warm mixture. It will gradually melt. Because the mixture will be whisked when it is reheated, the butter will be absorbed easily into the sauce.

Making a sauce of coating consistency.

Rubbing the surface of a sauce with butter to prevent a skin forming.

Thickening a sauce If a sauce tastes good but is too thin, it should be thickened with cornflour, arrowroot or kneaded butter (beurre manié) instead of by reduction which concentrates the flavour.

For cornflour or arrowroot, stir the powder into a small quantity of cold water or other liquid until dissolved. Pour it gradually into the boiling sauce, whisking constantly. Add enough for the sauce to thicken to the desired consistency and bring back to the boil.

Alternatively, knead together equal quantities of butter and flour and whisk this piece by piece into the boiling sauce until the desired consistency is reached. Simmer for a few minutes and remove from the heat. This will give a slightly richer texture to the sauce than thickening with cornflour or arrowroot.

Making gravy

The principle for making gravy for roast and fried meats is simple. The meat juices which congeal and slightly caramelise in the bottom of the roasting tin or frying pan are dissolved with hot liquid which can be water, stock or wine, or a combination of these.

Gravy for red meats should be dark brown and that for lighter meats or poultry a light golden colour. To add extra flavour to gravy from roasts cook a quartered onion and carrot, plus any bones, in the tin with the meat. If the juices start to burn on the bottom of the pan before roasting is finished add stock or water, using only a little at a time so the meat does not steam and lose its seared crust.

At the end of cooking pour excess fat from the roasting tin. The French like to leave a little fat in their gravy, particularly for dry meats such as veal and chicken, but this is a matter of taste. Usually you will find the juices remaining in the pan are sufficiently browned because of the high heat used. However, if they are still pale, you can continue cooking them on top of the stove.

Next add about 150 ml/$\frac{1}{4}$ pint of liquid per person. This can be water, stock, red or white wine, or a mixture. Boil hard, stirring to dissolve all the juices congealed on the bottom and sides of the pan, until the liquid is reduced by half. Strain the gravy into a saucepan, skim off excess fat, season and taste. If the gravy is still too thin continue boiling until the flavour is sufficiently concentrated.

How to make a bouquet garni

A bouquet garni or bunch of herbs is one of the key flavourings in French cooking. It consists of a small bay leaf, a sprig of fresh thyme and three to four stems of parsley. The parsley leaves are kept for chopping. Fold the parsley stems in half to enclose the thyme and bay leaf, then tie with string in a tight bundle. If fresh thyme is not available use $\frac{1}{4}$ teaspoon dried leaf thyme, and tie everything together in a piece of muslin. The bouquet garni is immersed in liquid during cooking, then discarded before serving. To make a large bouquet garni double the ingredients.

How to clarify butter

Clarifying eliminates the milky residue in butter, leaving only the pure fat. It is ideal for frying because it does not burn easily. Melt the butter in a saucepan over low heat. With a spoon skim and discard the froth from the surface of the butter. Carefully pour the clear melted butter into a bowl. Stop pouring the butter when you reach the milky residue in the bottom of the pan. Discard the milky residue.

How to use gelatine

Before adding to a hot liquid, gelatine must be softened. Sprinkle the powder over 2–3 tablespoons of water or other liquid as specified in the recipe. Never add the liquid to the gelatine. After this the gelatine must be dissolved by adding to a hot, but not boiling liquid, or by warming in a water bath. In either case the gelatine must be stirred until completely dissolved. Never let gelatine overheat or it will become stringy.

Stir a gelatine mixture from time to time while it cools. As soon as the liquid starts to thicken fold in any other ingredients such as whipped cream or egg whites. Pour into a prepared dish or mould and chill for two to four hours until set.

Pastry

How to line a flan tin If possible use a flan tin with a loose base so the flan can be removed easily. Grease the flan tin and roll out the dough 5 mm/$\frac{1}{4}$ in thick.

Wrap the dough around the rolling pin, lift it over the flan tin and unroll it. Let the dough rest over the edge of the tin, overlapping it slightly inside. Be careful not to stretch it. Gently lift the edges of the dough with one hand and press it well into the bottom corners of the tin with the other.

Roll the rolling pin over the top of the tin to cut off excess dough. Using your forefinger and thumb, press the dough evenly up the sides from the bottom to increase the height of the edge. Neaten the edge with your finger and thumb and flute it if you are making a sweet flan. Do not let the dough overlap the edge of the tin.

Prick the base of the shell thoroughly to prevent air bubbles forming during cooking.

How to line tartlet tins or boat moulds Grease the moulds and arrange them close together near the work surface. Roll out the dough 5 mm/$\frac{1}{4}$ in thick. Wrap the dough around the rolling pin, lift it and gently lay it on top of the moulds, being careful not to stretch it. Press the dough gently into the base of the moulds.

Roll the rolling pin over the tops of the moulds to trim the pastry. Using your forefinger and thumb, press the dough evenly up the sides of the mould from the bottom to increase the height of the edge. Neaten the edges with your finger and thumb. Do not let the dough overlap the edges of the moulds.

Prick the bottoms of the shells thoroughly to prevent air bubbles forming during cooking.

Baking blind Baking blind refers to the method of cooking an unfilled pastry case. Cut a circle of greaseproof paper 5 cm/2 in larger than the diameter of the flan tin. For tartlets, crumple small pieces of greaseproof paper. Line the pastry case with the paper, pressing it well into the corners. Fill the case three-quarters full with uncooked dried beans or rice to hold the dough in shape. Bake according to the recipe.

How to make egg glaze To colour pastry golden brown, brush with egg glaze before baking. Beat 1 egg with $\frac{1}{2}$ teaspoon salt until well mixed. The salt breaks down the egg white, making the glaze liquid. Just before baking, brush the pastry with a light coating of the glaze, taking care it does not drip down the sides and seal the pastry to the baking sheet.

How to Line a Flan Tin

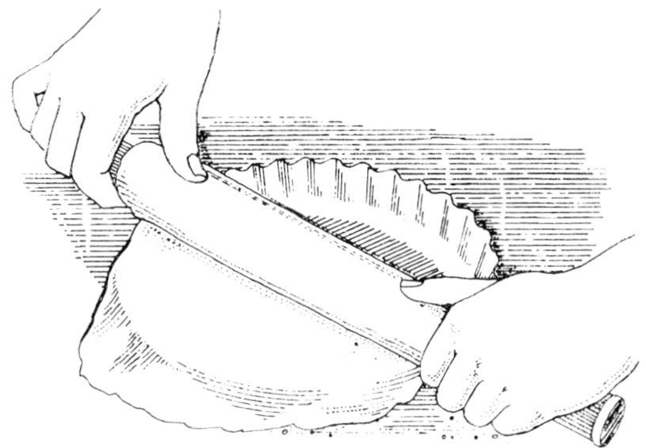

Wrap the rolled-out dough around the rolling pin and unroll over the flan tin.

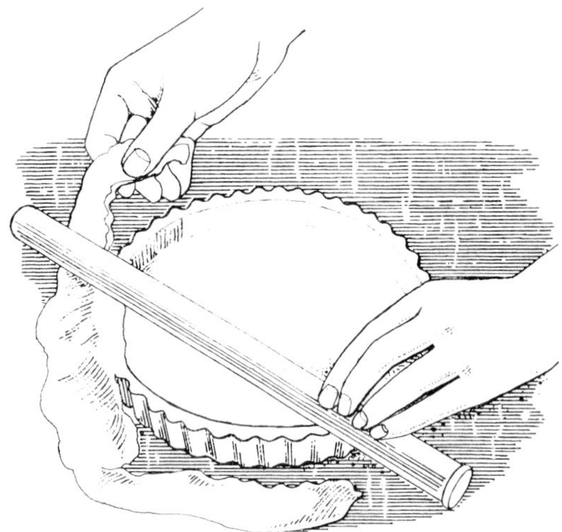

Roll the rolling pin over the top of the flan tin to cut off excess dough.

With your thumb and forefinger, press the dough up the sides of the flan tin.

How to peel, seed and chop tomatoes

Tomatoes must often be peeled and seeded before use because the skin and seeds would spoil the smooth texture of a sauce or stew.

Using a small knife, remove the core of each tomato. Cut a cross in the opposite end of the tomato, making a shallow cut to slit the skin but not the flesh. Put the tomatoes in a large bowl and pour over enough boiling water to cover. Leave for 10 to 15 seconds until the skin begins to pull away from the slit. Do not leave them for too long or they will start to cook. With a slotted spoon transfer the tomatoes immediately to a bowl of cold water. When cool, drain them and peel off the skin with a small knife; it will come away easily.

To remove the seeds, halve each tomato horizontally and hold over a bowl, squeezing out the seeds and juice without crushing the pulp.

Peeling and seeding tomatoes.

How to make lemon decorations

Lemons can be used to decorate a great number of sweet and savoury dishes and are particularly appropriate with fish. Other citrus fruits can be treated in the same way.

Wolf's Teeth Cut a thin slice from the top and bottom of the lemon, so the two halves will stand level. With a small pointed knife, cut a zig-zag line all round the lemon cutting to the centre of the fruit. Pull the two halves apart. These can be sprinkled with chopped parsley before serving. Lemon prepared in this way is very good served with a fish dish so that each person can squeeze over lemon juice to taste.

Fluted Lemon Slices Use a citrus stripper or canelle knife to cut lengthways grooves down the lemon. Try to space the grooves evenly. Cut the lemon across into thin slices or halve then slice.

Making wolf's teeth and lemon baskets.

How to use a piping bag

A piping bag is almost indispensable for shaping many biscuits as well as making meringues and piping decorative patterns of cream or mashed potato. It is quite simple to use a piping bag and after a little practice you will find that you can produce very professional results.

First put the required nozzle in the bag. Hold the bag, tip downwards, in your left hand and fold about 5 cm/2 in of the bag over your open hand. Gently spoon in the mixture; then unfold the top of the bag and twist it to close, pushing the mixture down the tube.

Hold the filled bag in your right hand, keeping the twisted top between thumb and first finger. Use the remaining fingers of your right hand to press the mixture in the bag. With the left hand support the bag without squeezing it. While piping, hold the bag slightly above the surface to be decorated so the nozzle does not actually touch it. Reverse the directions if you are left-handed.

Filling a piping bag with mixture.

Whipping egg whites to stiff peaks

Egg whites should be whipped until stiff but not dry. In order for them to whip properly, the whites, bowl and whisk must be completely free from any trace of water, grease or egg yolk. The French prefer to whip egg whites in a copper bowl, using a balloon whisk because they acquire greater density and volume than by any other method. The best alternative is to use an electric beater with a metal bowl.

Begin by whipping the whites at a low speed and when they become foamy and white increase the speed to maximum. The whites are beaten enough when they form a stiff peak when the whisk is lifted and the whites gather in the whisk and stick to it without falling. If overbeaten, the egg whites become dry and lumpy and cannot be folded together easily with other ingredients.

Whipping egg whites to stiff peaks.

Folding in

To preserve the lightness of the ingredients many mixtures are folded together rather than stirred or beaten. Whipped egg whites are folded into soufflé bases and some cake mixtures so they don't lose the air that makes them rise in the oven. In gelatine desserts, whipped cream is folded into the basic mixture so the cream doesn't separate due to overbeating. Flour and melted butter are folded into a genoese mixture so they do not cause the delicate egg mixture to lose its volume.

Two mixtures fold together most easily if their consistency is similar. If one ingredient is much lighter than the other, stir a little of it thoroughly into the heavier mixture. This procedure is especially helpful for folding egg whites into a base mixture to make soufflés. Then add the heavier mixture to the lighter one, so the heavier mixtures does not sit at the bottom of the bowl.

Use a wooden spatula or a large metal spoon for folding. Cut the spoon across the centre of the mixture, scraping the bottom of the bowl, and scooping the spoon under the mixture towards the left side of the bowl. At the same time, with the left hand, turn the bowl anti-clockwise. Reverse the directions if you are left-handed. This should be a synchronised movement: cut and scoop the spoon with one hand, turn the bowl with the other. In this way, the spoon reaches as great a volume of mixture as possible in one movement, so the mixture is folded quickly and the ingredients mixed easily, losing a minimum of air.

How to make caramel

Caramel is the last stage reached when boiling a sugar syrup. The syrup browns to a deep golden caramel just before it burns.

Always use a heavy saucepan to cook caramel or the syrup will cook unevenly, burning in some spots before it browns in others. Heat the sugar and water over low heat, shaking the pan occasionally, until the sugar is dissolved. Sugar syrup should never be stirred during cooking as it may crystallise before it cooks to the stage you want. When the sugar is dissolved, boil the syrup over high heat. At first it will boil rapidly, then the bubbles will break more slowly until the syrup turns golden at the edges of the pan. This is the start of caramelisation. When the caramel is golden brown it is mild and sweet. The darker it turns the stronger the flavour of the caramel until it starts to burn and becomes bitter. The caramel has reached this stage when it smokes. Caramel syrup changes colour fast, so watch it carefully, lifting it off the heat from time to time to control cooking. When it is deep golden, dip the base of the pan in cold water to stop cooking immediately.

Caramel reaches a very high temperature so take care when working with it. Use an oven glove to protect your hand from splashes and when adding warm water to make a caramel sauce, stand back as the mixture will splatter.

How to flame or flambé foods

Flaming is not just for spectacular show. At the same time as it burns off the alcohol, the flame toasts the dish and, if it contains sugar, helps to caramelise it. When the flame goes out only the essence of the brandy or liqueur will remain. Dishes must be flamed with a spirit which contains a high proportion of alcohol such as rum or brandy. Liqueurs such as Grand Marnier can be used alone or can be mixed with a higher proof liqueur for flaming.

Be sure the food you want to flame is very hot and heat the alcohol in a small saucepan until hot but not boiling. Stand back and turn your face from the flames, then light the heated spirit and pour it, flaming, over the food and baste the dish rapidly. If the dish was not hot enough, the flames will die at once. They should be left to go out naturally, but if the food starts to scorch, blow out the flame. Crêpes are especially prone to burn at the edges.

Using a water bath or bain marie

A water bath or bain marie is used for cooking food which needs a consistently low heat so that it is cooked in the centre without overcooking on the outside.

Set the cooking dish in a large shallow pan such as a roasting tin and fill with hot water to within one inch of the rim of the dish. Bring the water to the boil on top of the stove, then transfer the dish in the water bath to the oven. Start counting the cooking time from the moment when the bath is put in the oven.

Stocks and Soups

Simmer a few bones and vegetables in water and you'll have *stock*, a basic ingredient in many French soups, sauces and main dishes. Stock is simple and inexpensive to make at home. Don't regard it as just a tiresome intermediate preparation that leads nowhere. If you add a simple garnish like chopped fresh herbs or sliced mushrooms, you'll have a clear soup. For something more substantial, cook a few vegetables in the stock, as in French Onion Soup. More sophisticated is Consommé which is made of stock clarified with egg whites and simmered with beef and vegetables so it becomes sparkling clear and aromatic.

For a soup of completely different character, simmer chopped vegetables in stock, purée them and enrich the soup with milk, cream or butter to make a thickened soup. Bisque is a variation made with shellfish. Rice or potatoes give body to this type of soup, though its consistency should never approach the thickness of a sauce.

How to Make Stock

Stock depends on bones for most of its flavour and body – particularly veal bones which contain a good deal of gelatine. Chicken and other poultry bones have some gelatine also, as do fish bones. There are only two requirements for making good stock: the liquid must be skimmed often to remove grease and foam, particularly while coming to a boil, and it must be cooked at a low simmer – never boiled. If stock does boil, it becomes cloudy and acquires an unpleasant acrid taste.

Vegetables, notably onion and carrot, add flavour to all kinds of stock. Some benefit from the addition of a stick of celery, a bouquet garni and even a clove of garlic. In general, avoid strong ingredients like cabbage or turnip. Stock is never seasoned at the beginning of cooking. This is because the liquid is boiled to reduce it to half or less of its original volume and strong flavours – especially salt – can become overpowering. If you season stock at the end or when adding it to a dish, you can adjust the taste to suit the other ingredients.

How to Prepare Stock Ahead

Stock is easy to prepare ahead. Once the liquid has come to a boil and simmered an hour, you can interrupt cooking, cool the stock by placing the pot in a sink of cold running water and refrigerate it up to a day before continuing. After stock is cooked completely, strain it and cool quickly for it turns sour within a few hours at room temperature. Refrigerate it as soon as possible and never leave it in a warm kitchen. If stored in an aluminium pot, it can also turn sour. Stock freezes perfectly or it can be stored 1 to 2 days (for fish stock) or 2 to 3 days (for poultry and meat stock) in the refrigerator. To keep poultry and meat stock longer still, bring it to a boil and simmer 10 minutes before refrigerating again for a day or two.

How to Use Stock

As a general rule, white stock goes with light meats such as poultry, veal and pork. Brown stock is mainly for beef and lamb dishes. Uses of the other types are equally logical: fish stock for seafood, and chicken stock for poultry. But even if you have only one or two kinds of stock on hand, some substituting is still possible. Beef stock doubles for brown veal stock and chicken for white veal stock. Only fish stock has no substitute and even then a simple version can be made with clam juice.

Soup Garnishes

Fried croutons are the most common garnish for thickened soups. In France they are passed in a separate bowl to preserve their crispness. However, do not serve them with consommé because their fat clouds the soup. Ideal for serving with consommé are small poached eggs or shreds of leftover crepes. Miniature Cheese Puffs can be served separately. Most other garnishes suit either type of soup, so choose what you like. Croûtes of sliced bread that are toasted rather than fried can be topped with grated cheese before browning. Grated cheese can also be served separately

White Veal Stock

Fond Blanc de Veau

1.75to 2.5 kg/4 to 5 lb veal bones cracked or cut into 2 to 3 pieces
2 onions, quartered
2 carrots, quartered
2 celery sticks, cut into 5-cm/2-in pieces
1 large bouquet garni
10 peppercorns
1 clove of garlic
3 to 3.5 litres/5 to 6 pints water

If you don't have a heavy cleaver ask the butcher to crack or cut the bones. Place all the ingredients into a large saucepan. Slowly bring to the boil over a period of 20–30 minutes, skimming occasionally. Add more water during cooking to keep the bones covered. Stock should reduce very slowly to about 2 litres/3½ pints. Strain the stock and taste. If not well flavoured boil to reduce and concentrate the flavour.

Cool the stock quickly by placing pot in a sink of cold running water, then chill. When cold, skim solidified fat off the top. White veal stock can be made 2 to 3 days ahead, covered and refrigerated or frozen. After 3 days of refrigeration boil for 10 minutes and cool. Stock can then be refrigerated for another 1 to 2 days. **Makes 2 litres/3½ pints**

Chicken Stock

Fond de Volaille

Make light stock by poaching a whole chicken and use the chicken meat for another recipe.

1 (1.5-kg/3-lb) chicken wings or one whole chicken
2 onions, quartered
2 carrots, quartered
2 sticks celery, roughly chopped
1 large bouquet garni
10 peppercorns
1 clove garlic
2 litres/3½ pints water

Place all the ingredients in a large saucepan; the chicken should be covered with water. Bring slowly to the boil over a period of 20–30 minutes, skimming frequently. If using chicken wings, reduce the heat and simmer uncovered for 3 to 4 hours, skimming occasionally. If using a whole chicken, remove the chicken after 1–1½ hours when the thigh is tender when pierced with a skewer, strip the meat from the bones and return the bones to the pot. Add more water, if necessary, to keep the bones covered and continue to cook for a further 2–3 hours. The chicken meat may be used in another dish. Strain the stock and taste; if not well flavoured, boil to reduce and concentrate the flavour.

Cool the stock quickly by placing the pan in a sink of cold running water and store in the refrigerator. When cold skim solidified fat off the top. Chicken stock can be made 2 to 3 days ahead, covered and refrigerated or frozen. After 3 days of refrigeration, boil stock for 10 minutes and cool. Stock can then be refrigerated for another 1 or 2 days. **Makes 1.25 litres/2¼ pints**

Variation

Turkey Stock *(Fond de Dinde)*
Substitute 1.5 kg/3 lb raw turkey wings for the chicken.

Brown Veal Stock

Use roasted veal bones and cut up vegetables.

Skim fat and foam from stock occasionally.

Brown Veal Stock

Fond Brun de Veau

1.75 to 2.25 kg/4 to 5 lb veal bones, cracked or cut in 2 or 3 pieces
2 onions, quartered
2 carrots, quartered
2 sticks celery, roughly chopped
1 large bouquet garni
10 peppercorns
1 clove garlic
1 tablespoon concentrated tomato purée
3–3.5 litres/5–6 pints water
$\frac{1}{2}$ onion (optional)

Preheat oven to hot (230 C, 450 F, gas 8). If you don't have a heavy cleaver, ask the butcher to crack or cut the bones for you. Place the bones in a roasting tin and roast for 30 to 40 minutes until browned, turning the bones from time to time so that they brown evenly. Stir in the carrot and celery. Continue roasting until vegetables are browned.

Transfer the bones and vegetables from the roasting tin to a large saucepan, leaving any fat in the tin. Add the bouquet garni, peppercorns, garlic and tomato purée to the bones and vegetables and pour over the water. Slowly bring to the boil, taking 20 to 30 minutes and skimming often. To add more colour, singe the cut part of half an onion on a preheated electric hot plate or over a gas flame. Add to the stock. Reduce the heat and simmer uncovered for 4 to 5 hours, skimming occasionally. Add more water during cooking as necessary to keep the bones covered. The stock should reduce very slowly to about 2 litres/$3\frac{1}{2}$ pints. Strain and taste. If not well flavoured, boil to reduce and concentrate the flavour.

Cool quickly by placing the saucepan in a sink of cold running water then chill in the refrigerator. When cold, skim the solidified fat off the top. Brown veal stock can be made 2 to 3 days ahead, covered and chilled or frozen. After 3 days of refrigeration, boil stock 10 minutes and cool. Stock can then be refrigerated another 1 or 2 days. **Makes 2 litres/$3\frac{1}{2}$ pints**

Variation

Brown Beef Stock *Fond Brun de Boeuf*
Substitute beef bones for veal bones. Brown beef stock has a milder flavour than brown veal stock. It also has less body because it contains less gelatine. Brown beef stock is often used to make rich sauces for beef and game.

Fish Stock

Fumet de Poisson

Do not let fish stock boil, or it will taste bitter.

15 g/½ oz butter
1 medium onion, sliced
675 g/1½ lb fish bones and trimmings, broken into pieces
1 litre/1¾ pints water
10 peppercorns
1 bouquet garni
250 ml/8 fl oz dry white wine *or* the juice of ½ lemon (optional)

Melt the butter in a large pan and stir in the onion. Cook over medium heat until the onion is soft but not browned. Add the fish bones etc, water, peppercorns, bouquet garni and wine or lemon juice. The liquid should almost cover the fish. Do not add fish skins or the stock will darken. Slowly bring to the boil, skimming frequently. Reduce the heat and simmer uncovered for 20 minutes. Strain, cool and refrigerate. Fish stock can be made 1 to 2 days ahead, covered and chilled or frozen. **Makes about 1 litre/1¾ pints**

Rouille Sauce

Sauce Rouille

A spicy sauce to spread on fried bread and serve with a fish soup.

1 medium slice bread, crusts removed
1 small red chilli, chopped
3–4 cloves garlic, crushed
1 egg yolk
salt and pepper
6 tablespoons olive oil

Soak the bread in 2 tablespoons of water and squeeze dry. Purée the bread, chilli, garlic, egg yolk and a little salt with 2 tablespoons olive oil in a liquidiser or food processor. With the liquidiser on medium speed gradually add the remaining olive oil. Taste and add more salt and pepper if necessary.

Prawn Bisque

Bisque de Crevettes

The whole prawn is used in this rich, satisfying soup.

25 g/1 oz butter
½ carrot, diced
½ onion, diced
1 bouquet garni
675 g/1½ lb unpeeled prawns
6 tablespoons white wine
1 tablespoon brandy
1.15 litres/2 pints white veal stock (page 19) *or* chicken stock (page 19) *or* fish stock (page 20)
25 g/1 oz long-grain rice
salt and pepper
1 tablespoon sherry or Madeira
3 tablespoons single cream
pinch cayenne pepper
croûtons for serving (page 22)

Melt 15 g/½ oz of the butter in a large saucepan and stir in the carrot, onion and bouquet garni. Cover and cook over a low heat for 5 to 7 minutes until the vegetables are soft but not browned. Stir in the prawns and cook for a further 1 to 2 minutes, stirring occasionally. Pour in the wine and brandy and boil for 1 minute to reduce the liquid. Add 600 ml/1 pint stock. Simmer for 2 to 3 minutes until the prawns are just tender. Remove from the heat, cool slightly, lift out 12 prawns and peel them, discarding the intestinal vein, and set aside. Return the shells to the saucepan. Add the remaining stock and remove and reserve the bouquet garni, then purée the prawn and vegetable mixture with the liquid in a liquidiser or food processor.

Return the mixture to the pan with the bouquet garni and stir in the rice, salt and pepper. Cover the pan and simmer for 15 to 20 minutes then remove and discard the bouquet garni. Purée the mixture again in a liquidiser or food processor then press the soup through a fine sieve. Coarsely chop the reserved prawns. Bring the soup to a boil, add the sherry or Madeira and cream. Simmer for 2 minutes then remove the soup from the heat. Season with cayenne pepper and add the remaining butter in small pieces. Taste and adjust the seasoning. Serve in soup bowls with a spoonful of chopped prawns on top accompanied by croûtons. **Serves 6**

Mediterranean Fish Soup

Bouillabaisse

The more kinds of fish used the more interesting the flavour, so use at least five different varieties.

1.5 kg/3 lb white fish such as whiting, bass, red mullet, haddock or monkfish
1 kg/2 lb oily fish such as eel or mackerel
2 large crabs, cooked
1 large lobster, cooked
175 ml/6 fl oz olive oil
2 medium onions, sliced
the white part of 2 leeks, sliced
2 sticks of celery, sliced
3 tomatoes, peeled, seeded and chopped
3–4 cloves garlic, crushed
1 bouquet garni
thin strip of orange peel
2 sprigs fresh fennel or 1 teaspoon dried fennel
¼ teaspoon saffron strands
salt and pepper to taste
To finish
1 tablespoon concentrated tomato purée
1 tablespoon Pernod
3 tablespoons chopped parsley

Cut the fish into large chunks, reserving heads and tails. Place the heads and tails in a saucepan and cover with 2 litres/3½ pints water. Bring to the boil and simmer gently for 15 minutes then strain. With a cleaver chop the crabs and lobster in pieces, shells included. Discard the head, sac and intestinal veins of the lobster and the spongy finger-like gills of the crabs. Heat the olive oil in a large saucepan and use to sauté the onions, leeks and celery until soft but not browned. Add the fish stock, tomatoes, garlic, bouquet garni, orange peel and fennel then sprinkle the saffron, salt and pepper over the mixture. Bring to the boil, reduce the heat and simmer for 30–45 minutes.

Bring the broth to the boil 20 minutes before serving time and add the oily fish and shellfish. Boil rapidly for 7 minutes. Do not stir but shake the pan occasionally to prevent sticking. Lay the white fish on top of the mixture and boil for a further 5 to 8 minutes until the fish begins to flake easily. If necessary add water to keep the fish covered. Keep the liquid at a rolling boil during the entire cooking time so that the oil emulsifies with broth and does not float on the surface.

Remove from the heat and transfer the fish to a warm plate, arranging each type separately. Cover with foil and keep warm. Whisk the tomato purée and Pernod into the hot broth and adjust the seasoning. Pour the broth into a tureen and sprinkle the broth and the fish pieces with parsley. Serve immediately, letting each guest help himself to fish and then spoon broth over it. Serve with croûtes (page 22) and Rouille Sauce (page 20). Mediterranean Fish Soup can also be served as 2 separate courses of soup and fish. **Serves 8–10**

French Onion Soup

Soup a l'Oignon

3 lb/1.5 kg strong onions
50 g/2 oz butter
1 teaspoon sugar
1.15 litres/2 pints white veal stock (page 19) *or* brown beef stock (page 18)
salt and pepper
½ stick French bread cut in 1-cm/½-in slices
25 g/1 oz grated Parmesan cheese
75 g/3 oz grated Gruyère cheese
25 g/1 oz melted butter

Slice all but one of the onions and add to 40 g/1½ oz of the butter in a large saucepan. Sauté over a low heat for 15 to 20 minutes, stirring frequently until the onions are golden. Be careful not to burn them. Peel the whole onion, cut a thin slice off the top and bottom and dip the cut ends in sugar. Melt the remaining butter in a small saucepan and cook the whole onion over low heat until it caramelises at both ends. Add the whole onion to the sliced onions and continue to cook over a low heat until the sliced onions are dark brown. Add the stock, salt and pepper, bring to the boil then simmer for 10 to 15 minutes. Discard the whole onion. Taste the soup for seasoning. French onion soup can be made to this point 2 to 3 days ahead, covered and then chilled.

Just before serving preheat the grill. Place bread slices on a baking sheet and grill until lightly browned. Place 2 to 3 slices of toasted bread in individual ovenproof bowls and spoon in the soup. Mix the Parmesan and Gruyère cheeses together and sprinkle a thick layer of cheese over each serving, followed by a little of the melted butter. Grill until brown and bubbling. **Serves 4**

Fresh Pea Soup

Potage St Germain

(Illustrated opposite)
Like dill with cucumber, mint with peas is a classic combination

3 sprigs fresh mint
275 g/10 oz fresh, shelled or frozen peas
900 ml/1½ pints chicken stock (page 19)
salt and pepper
150 ml/¼ pint single cream
1 teaspoon sugar (optional)
25 g/1 oz butter cut in small pieces

Coarsely chop one of the sprigs of mint then set aside. In a large saucepan bring the stock to the boil along with the remaining mint and salt and pepper to taste. Add 225 g/8 oz of the peas and simmer uncovered for 15 to 20 minutes until the peas are very tender. Fresh peas may take longer than frozen ones depending on their size.

Discard the cooked mint then purée the peas and stock in a liquidiser or food processor. Strain to remove any skins. Stir in half the cream. Bring the soup to the boil, adjust the seasoning and add sugar if desired. In a small saucepan bring 300 ml/½ pint water to the boil and add the remaining peas. Cook for 3–10 minutes until just tender, then drain. Remove the soup from the heat and stir in the butter until melted. Spoon into bowls and swirl a spoonful of cream into each one. Sprinkle with peas and chopped mint and serve at once. **Serves 4**

Fresh Pea Soup with Miniature Cheese Puffs (above).

Soup Garnishes

Miniature Cheese Puffs *Petits Choux au Fromage*

choux pastry (page 117, made with 50 g/2 oz flour)
25 g/1 oz grated Parmesan cheese

Preheat the oven to moderately hot (200 C, 400 F, gas 6). Lightly grease a baking sheet.

Prepare the choux pastry, beating in the cheese after adding the eggs. Spoon the mixture into a piping bag fitted with a 3-mm/⅛-in plain nozzle. Pipe small mounds onto the prepared baking sheet. Bake for 12 to 15 minutes until crisp and browned. **Makes about 30**

Croûtes *Croûtes*

150 ml/¼ pint olive oil
1 long French loaf, cut in 20 diagonal slices
1 clove garlic

Heat the olive oil in a frying pan until very hot. Add half the bread slices and toss until they are evenly browned. Remove and drain on absorbent kitchen paper. Repeat with the remaining slices of bread. Rub each croûte with the cut side of a half clove of garlic.

Croutons *Croûtons*

3 slices white bread, crusts removed
3 tablespoons vegetable oil
40 g/1½ oz butter

Cut the bread into small cubes. In a frying pan, heat the oil and butter until very hot. Add the bread and shake the frying pan over a medium heat until the croûtons are evenly browned. Remove and drain on absorbent kitchen paper.

Consommé

Consommé

Good consommé is sparkling clear. Egg whites are used to filter out any cloudiness.

1.5 litres/$2\frac{1}{2}$ pints brown beef stock (page 18) *or* chicken stock (page 19)
15 g/$\frac{1}{2}$ oz powdered gelatine (optional)
salt and pepper
350 g/12 oz very lean beef, minced
2 carrots, chopped
2 leeks, chopped
2 sticks celery, chopped
2 tomatoes, quartered
3 egg whites
3 tablespoons Madeira or sherry
julienne, brunoise, madrilène *or* niçoise garnish (see below)

Chill the stock until partially set and skim the fat from the surface. If the stock doesn't set, and you wish to serve jellied consommé, reserve 6 tablespoons to soften the gelatine later. In a large pan, melt the rest of the stock and remove any remaining traces of fat by quickly placing strips of absorbent kitchen paper over the surface. Remove from the heat and cool. Season to taste with salt and pepper then stir in the beef, carrots, leeks, celery and tomatoes. Whisk the egg whites until frothy and stir into the cool stock. Bring slowly to the boil, stirring constantly for 10 to 15 minutes. Stop stirring as soon as the stock looks milky as this means that the egg whites are cooked. With the pan over medium heat let the cooked egg white particles rise undisturbed to the surface, forming a filter. Reduce the heat to low. Use a ladle to make a small hole in the egg-white filter so that the broth can bubble through. Don't make more than one hole or the filter may break. If the stock didn't partially set when chilled, sprinkle the gelatine over the 6 tablespoons reserved stock and leave to stand for 5 minutes until spongy. Carefully spoon the spongy gelatine through the hole in the filter and simmer for 2 to 3 minutes to dissolve. Remove the consommé from the heat. Add the Madeira or sherry through the hole in the filter. More seasoning added at this point may cloud the consommé.

Place a scalded tea-towel over a colander and place this over a large bowl. Ladle half the consommé over the tea-towel, then slide in the filter with the remaining consommé. Let the consommé strain slowly without pressing it through. The colander should not touch the liquid so there is room for liquid to drain. If the consommé is not sparkling clear, strain it again. Prepare the garnish (see below). To serve hot consommé, bring almost to a boil and add the garnish just before serving. Do not cook the garnishes in the consommé as they will cloud it. For cold consommé, refrigerate until slightly set. Just before serving, stir with a fork; spoon into chilled bowls and top with garnish. **Serves 4**

Garnishes

Julienne Garnish for Beef Consommé (*Garniture pour Consommé Julienne*) Cut 1 small carrot, 1 stick celery, 1 small white turnip and the white part of 1 small leek into very thin strips. Simmer in 250 ml/8 fl oz consommé for 5 to 8 minutes until tender. Drain and add to the consommé.

Niçoise Garnish for Beef or Chicken Consommé (*Garniture pour Consommé Niçoise*) Cut 1 small potato and 4 green beans into small dice. Simmer in 250 ml/8 fl oz consommé for 4 to 5 minutes or until tender then drain. Peel, deseed and dice 1 tomato (page 14). Add vegetables to the consommé just before serving.

Madrilène Garnish for Beef or Chicken Consommé (*Garniture pour Consommé Madrilène*) Just before serving, peel, seed and cut 2 tomatoes in thin strips. Add to the consommé.

Starters

French cookbooks rarely devote much space to starters – they leave them to the cook's imagination. Once you know a few basic recipes you can create your own delicious starters.

When planning a starter keep one rule in mind: make it light and serve small portions. This is the ideal course to introduce an expensive ingredient as it will only be needed in small quantities and will provide an impressive beginning to the meal. Foie gras (fattened goose liver), for example, will be shown to best advantage when served in small amounts like this. You can also use up pieces of meat or fish that would not be enough for a main course.

Don't think you need to spend hours on preparation. Some of the best starters are so simple there are no recipes to describe them. For instance, you can serve thinly sliced cooked or Parma ham with gherkins, green or black olives, sliced rye bread and butter. Smoked fish, whether salmon, trout, mackerel or eel, is very popular, accompanied by buttered wholemeal bread and wedges of lemon. Leftover fish or chicken can be mixed with mayonnaise and served on lettuce leaves. Some starters such as the Country Terrine could be served in slightly larger quantities as a light main course. Conversely, many recipes in other sections of the book would make excellent starters.

Getting Ahead

Because so many meat and vegetable starters are served cold, they can be prepared ahead. Many are improved if the flavours have time to blend and mature, particularly pâtés and terrines.

Pastries and crêpes, which are best made the same day, have the advantage of needing ingredients that are generally at hand – flour, butter, eggs and milk. Fillings can range from simple scrambled eggs to luxuries such as lobster, shrimps, oysters or asparagus. Because they are invariably mixed with mayonnaise or white sauce, a little goes a long way.

How to Serve Starters

Starters should act as an invitation, but must not overwhelm the dishes to follow. Be careful not to over-season and take time on presentation. For cocktails make pastries all the same size and arrange them in a grand display on a platter. A touch here and there of black olive, tomato, green pepper or parsley can make all the difference. Add colour to cold starters with lettuce leaves or lemon decorations if appropriate.

Quiche Lorraine

Quiche Lorraine

For a less rich filling, substitute milk for half the cream

shortcrust pastry (page 112), made with 200 g/7 oz flour
3 eggs
350 ml/12 fl oz single cream
salt and pepper
pinch of grated nutmeg
15 g/½ oz butter
4 rashers lean bacon, diced
75 g/3 oz Cheddar or Gruyère cheese, diced

Chill the pastry in the refrigerator for at least 30 minutes before using. Set the oven at moderately hot (200 C, 400 F, gas 6). Roll out the chilled pastry to a thickness of ¼ in/5 mm and use to line a 9-in/23-cm flan tin (page 13). Refrigerate until the pastry is firm, then bake blind for 15 minutes or until cooked but not completely browned. Allow to cool slightly in the flan tin.

Reduce the oven temperature to 190 C, 375 F, gas 5 and place a baking sheet in the oven to heat. Beat the eggs with the cream, seasoning and nutmeg. Melt the butter in a small frying pan and sauté the bacon until browned. Sprinkle the bacon and cheese over the bottom of the pastry case, place the flan tin on the hot baking tray and pour the egg mixture over the bacon and cheese. Bake for 35 to 40 minutes until the filling is set and golden brown. Do not overcook otherwise the filling will curdle. Serve hot or at room temperature. **Serves 6–8**

Variation

Onion Quiche (*Quiche à l'Oignon*) Omit the bacon and cheese. Thinly slice 4 large onions. Melt 25 g/1 oz butter in a heavy saucepan, stir in the onion and season to taste with salt and pepper. Press a piece of buttered foil on top of the onion, cover the pan and cook over very low heat, stirring occasionally, for 20 to 30 minutes until soft but not browned. Allow to cool slightly, then spread in the pastry case. Pour the egg mixture over the onion and continue as for Quiche Lorraine.

Quiches can be made 1 day ahead but not more because the pastry will become soggy. Cover tightly and refrigerate until wanted. Reheat chilled quiche in a moderate oven (180 C, 350 F, gas 4).

Sausage in Brioche

Saucisson en Brioche

(Illustrated on page 27)
If you prefer more meat increase the number of sausages to four.

1 quantity brioche dough (page 121)
2 French or Polish garlic sausages (about 1.25 kg/1½ lb)
beaten egg to glaze

Prepare the brioche dough and leave to rise at room temperature. Refrigerate for 30 minutes before rolling out. If the sausage is already cooked remove the skin, if not cooked poach in barely simmering water for about 20 minutes, then drain, cool and remove the skin.

Grease two 23 × 13 × 10-cm/9 × 5 × 4-in loaf tins. Roll out the dough to a 46 × 18-cm/18 × 7-in rectangle. Place the sausages lengthwise along the centre of the dough. Wrap the dough round the sausages and pinch the edges to seal. Turn seamed side down and cut between the sausages. Pinch the ends of each roll to seal and place in the prepared tins. Cover with a clean damp tea-towel and leave to rise at room temperature for 25–30 minutes until the tins are almost full. Do not let the dough become too warm while rising or the butter will melt from the dough.

Preheat the oven to moderately hot (200 C, 400 F, gas 6). Brush the loaves with beaten egg to glaze and bake for 40 to 45 minutes until the brioche is well browned and starts to shrink away from the sides of the tin. Turn out the loaves and leave to cool on a wire rack. Serve cut into 2.5-cm/1 in slices, discarding the ends. **Serves 15–20**

Sausage in Brioche (above) and Country Terrine (page 29).

Mushroom Crêpes

Crêpes aux champignons

Always let batter stand 1 to 2 hours before cooking as it improves the texture of the crêpes.

CRÊPES

150 g/5 oz plain flour
¼ teaspoon salt
350 ml/12 fl oz milk
3 eggs
2 tablespoons melted butter or vegetable oil
4 tablespoons clarified butter (page 12) *or* vegetable oil for frying

FILLING

250 g/12 oz large mushrooms, diced
40 g/1½ oz butter
juice of ½ lemon
salt and pepper
thick basic white sauce (page 69) made with 600 ml/1 pint milk
pinch of nutmeg
6 tablespoons milk
6 tablespoons single cream
75 g/3 oz grated Gruyère or Cheddar cheese *or* 25 g/1 oz Parmesan cheese

First make the crêpes. Sift the flour into a large bowl. Make a well in the centre of the flour and add half the milk. Gradually whisk in the flour to make a smooth batter, then whisk in the eggs. Do not overbeat as the batter will become elastic and the crêpes will be tough. Stir in the melted butter or oil with half the remaining milk. Cover and leave the batter to stand for 1 to 2 hours. Just before using, stir in enough of the remaining milk to make the batter the consistency of thin cream.

Brush an 18-cm/7-in crêpe or frying pan with clarified butter or oil. Heat until a drop of batter sprinkled in the pan sizzles. Pour 2 to 3 tablespoons of batter into the pan, turning quickly to coat the bottom evenly. Cook over medium heat until the crêpe is browned on the bottom. Turn with a metal spatula, brown the other side and turn onto a plate. Continue with the remaining batter, greasing the pan only when the crêpes begin to stick. Pile the cooked crêpes on top of each other to keep the bottom ones moist and warm. If making the crêpes ahead, layer with greaseproof paper, cover and refrigerate for up to 3 days or freeze.

Place 5 mm/¼ in of water in a medium saucepan and add the mushrooms, 25 g/1 oz of the butter, the lemon juice and salt and pepper to taste. Cover and cook over high heat for 5 minutes until the liquid boils to the top of the pan and the mushrooms are tender. Cool. Prepare the white sauce and stir in the cooking liquid from the mushrooms. Season to taste with salt, pepper and nutmeg. Stir half the sauce into the mushrooms. Spoon a tablespoon of mushroom mixture on to the centre of each crêpe and roll into cigar shapes. Arrange the rolled crêpes in a greased ovenproof dish.

Stir the milk and cream into the remaining sauce. Reheat and check the seasoning. Pour the sauce over the crêpes and sprinkle with grated cheese. Melt the remaining butter and sprinkle over the grated cheese. Place under a hot grill until bubbling and browned. **Serves 6–8**

Chicken Liver Pâté

Pâté de Foies de Volailles

A delicious hors d'oeuvre to be served with toast triangles, bread or crispbread.

175 g/6 oz butter
1 onion, chopped
225 g/8 oz chicken livers
2 shallots, finely chopped
1 clove garlic, crushed
salt and pepper
2 tablespoons brandy
50 g/2 oz clarified butter (page 12) to finish (optional)

Melt 40 g/1½ oz of the butter in a medium frying pan, stir in the onion and cook over a low heat until soft but not browned. Stir in the chicken livers and continue cooking over medium heat for 2 to 3 minutes until browned on all sides but pink in the centre. Stir in the shallots, garlic and seasoning, reduce the heat and cook for a further minute. Remove from the heat and cool slightly. Purée the mixture in a liquidiser or food processor or press it through a sieve. Cool until lukewarm, then beat in the remaining butter and brandy. Taste and adjust the seasoning. Spoon the pâté into 4 ramekin dishes. Spoon the clarified butter over the top, if using.

Chicken Liver Pâté can be made in advance and refrigerated. It will keep for 4 days or up to a week if the butter topping is used, as this helps prevent a crust forming. **Serves 4–6**

Country Terrine

Terrine de Campagne

(Illustrated on page 27)

225 g/8 oz bacon, diced
15 g/½ oz butter
1 onion, chopped
450 g/1 lb pork sausagemeat
225 g/8 oz veal, minced
225 g/8 oz chicken livers, finely chopped
2 cloves garlic, finely chopped
¼ teaspoon ground allspice
pinch ground cloves
pinch nutmeg
2 small eggs, lightly beaten
6 tablespoons single cream (optional)
2 tablespoons brandy
salt and pepper
100 g/4 oz shelled pistachios blanched and peeled
1 thick slice ham (about 225 g/8 oz), cut in strips
1 bay leaf
1 sprig fresh thyme *or* ½ teaspoon dried thyme
2 to 3 tablespoons water
40 g/1½ oz flour

Line a 2-litre/3½-pint terrine or deep casserole with the bacon, reserving a few slices for the top. Preheat the oven to moderate (180 C, 350 F, gas 4). Melt the butter in a small saucepan and stir in the onion. Sauté until soft but not browned, then allow to cool. Mix the sautéed onion with the sausagemeat, veal, chicken livers, garlic, spices, eggs, cream, if using, brandy and salt and pepper to taste and beat thoroughly. Fry a small piece of mixture and taste for seasoning: it should be very spicy.

Spread a third of the mixture in the prepared terrine and then place the pistachios and strips of ham lengthwise over the mixture. Repeat this process and finally cover with the remaining meat mixture. Spread the remaining bacon slices over the top then cover with a lid. Mix the flour gently with the water to make a paste and spread this around the edge of the lid to seal the terrine. Place terrine in a water bath (page 16), bring to the boil on top of the stove then transfer to oven. Bake for 1½ hours or until a skewer inserted in the centre is hot to the touch 30 seconds after it has been withdrawn.

Remove the cooked terrine from the oven and leave until warm, then remove the flour and water paste and lid. Press the terrine with a board or plate weighted with a 1-kg/2-lb weight until the terrine is cool. Refrigerate for up to 7 days before serving; the flavour will continue to develop for a few days. Serve from the terrine or unmould and cut in slices. **Serves 8**

Ham and Parsley Mould

Jambon Persillé

(Illustrated on front endpaper)
Mild-cured country ham is the best kind to use for this dish, but other kinds can also be used successfully.

2 knuckle joints of ham (total weight about 2.25 kg/5 lb)
1 calf's or pig's trotter, split
225 g/8 oz veal bones
1 large bouquet garni
6 peppercorns tied in cheesecloth
½ bottle dry white wine
2 teaspoons white wine vinegar
1 tablespoon chopped parsley
salt and pepper

Cut the ham into cubes, reserving the bones and set the meat aside. Blanch the calf's or pig's trotter by covering with cold water, bringing it to the boil and simmering for 5 minutes. Drain. In a large saucepan place the ham and veal bones, the calf's or pig's trotter, bouquet garni, bag of peppercorns and wine. Add enough water to just cover the bones. Cover with a lid, bring slowly to the boil, reduce the heat and simmer gently for 3 hours. Add the cubed ham and simmer for a further hour, skimming frequently to remove any fat which rises to the surface. Remove from the heat and cool slightly.

Place the warm ham in a large bowl and discard the calf's or pig's trotter. Simmer the cooking liquid with the bones, uncovered, until reduced to about 900 ml/1½ pints. Strain through a sieve lined with muslin into a large bowl. Stir in the vinegar and parsley and season to taste with salt and pepper, bearing in mind that the ham may have made it salty enough already. Skim off any fat as it rises to the surface. Pull apart the pieces of ham and pile into a deep 1.75-litre/3-pint bowl. Spoon the parsley liquid over the pieces of meat and stir to coat completely. Cover and chill for 3 to 4 hours until set. Unmould on to a serving plate and serve cut in wedges. **Serves 8–10**

Note 15 g/½ oz powdered gelatine may be used to set the mould instead of the veal bones and calf's or pig's trotter. Soften in 2 tablespoons water then dissolve in the strained stock.

Aubergine Charlotte

Charlotte d'Aubergines

The tart flavour of yogurt perfectly balances the richness of aubergines in this mould.

3 to 4 aubergines (about 1 kg/2 lb)
salt and pepper
250 ml/8 fl oz olive oil
1 medium onion, finely chopped
1 clove garlic, crushed
10 tomatoes (about 1 kg/2 lb), peeled, seeded and chopped
250 ml/8 fl oz natural yogurt
250 ml/8 fl oz stock

Wipe the aubergines and trim off the stems. Cut them into 1-cm/½-in slices, then sprinkle with salt and leave to stand for 30 minutes. Drain the aubergines, rinse with cold water and pat dry on absorbent kitchen paper. Heat 2 tablespoons of the olive oil in a large frying pan. Add the onion and sauté until soft and lightly browned, stirring frequently. Add the garlic, tomatoes, salt and pepper to the onions in the pan and cook the mixture over medium heat, stirring from time to time for 20 to 30 minutes until the mixture is thick and pulpy. Taste and adjust the seasoning. Put aside about one-third of the tomato mixture for the sauce. Heat 2 tablespoons of the remaining olive oil in a large frying pan and brown the aubergine slices on both sides in several batches, adding more oil as necessary.

Arrange a layer of overlapping aubergine slices in a 1-litre/1¾-pint charlotte mould or 20-cm/8-in round cake tin and spread with a little tomato mixture and some of the yogurt. Continue the layers until all aubergine slices and yogurt are used up, ending with a layer of aubergines. Mix the reserved tomato mixture with the stock. Set the oven at moderate (180 C, 350 F, gas 4). Cover the mould with foil and bake for 40 to 50 minutes until a skewer inserted in the centre is still hot to the touch 30 seconds after being withdrawn. To serve hot, cool the charlotte slightly, then unmould on to a platter. Bring the tomato mixture to a boil in a medium saucepan, taste for seasoning and spoon around the base of the mould. To serve at room temperature let the charlotte cool and unmould a short time before serving; spoon the cooled sauce around the base. **Serves 6**

Aubergine Charlotte

Overlap browned aubergine slices in a charlotte mould.

Serve hot or at room temperature.

Fish

Ask the top Paris chefs what foods they enjoy preparing most and all will put fish and shellfish high on their lists. What are their reasons? First, the delicate, lean flesh of seafood makes it the perfect companion for French cuisine's richest sauces. And second, the short cooking time makes seafood easy to prepare to order, so it can be served straight from the pan.

How to Choose Fish

For the freshest fish, buy as the French do – without a shopping list so you can take advantage of the best the fishmonger has to offer. It is quite simple to recognise fresh fish. It should look good, have bright eyes and firm, moist flesh. Stale fish always looks tired and flabby and its strong smell is unmistakable.

If you cannot choose until you reach the shop, how can you know whether you'll find the fish called for in the recipe? The great advantage of fish cookery is that many fish are interchangeable. When you cannot find the sole fillets called for in a recipe you can use plaice or turbot. Most fish fall into two categories: white fish like sole and cod, and oily fish such as salmon and mackerel.

How to Prepare Fish for Cooking

Fish are usually sold cleaned and scaled. If any scales remain, scrape them off with a serrated knife, working from tail to head. The French usually leave on the heads of small fish such as trout, though you may remove them if you prefer. Trim the tails to a 'V' with scissors and cut off all the fins. Check fillets to be sure no bones remain by running a finger across the flesh. Wash the fish thoroughly in cold water, making sure the stomach cavity and gills are clean. Dry well on absorbent kitchen paper.

How to Tell When Fish is Cooked

Fish is delicate – so are shellfish, despite their tough shells. To keep it juicy, no matter what the cooking method, there is one important rule to remember: seafood must never be overcooked. If overdone, fish becomes soft, dry and tasteless. Shellfish such as shrimps can go soft and others such as scallops, lobster and mussels become unpleasantly tough and stringy.

As a fish cooks, three major transformations take place: its appearance changes from transparent to opaque, its temperature from cold to hot, and its texture from cohesive to flaky. To test small whole fish, fish fillets or scallops, poke the thickest part gently with a knife to see that no transparent centre remains and the flesh flakes quite easily. If so, the fish is cooked. For very large fish, you can use a meat thermometer which will register 71 to 74 C/160 to 165 F when the fish is done. Shellfish cooked in their shells must be judged by the time given in the recipe, because they cannot be tested.

Whatever the fish, remember that a few extra minutes means the difference between being done and overcooked. Begin testing early and, if in doubt, undercook slightly.

How to Serve Fish

At the beginning of this century in France, fish was always followed by a meat course, but today the French serve fish either as a starter or as a main course. Almost no accompaniment is needed with a fish starter. Lemon decorations (page 14) or parsley sprigs are possible, although neither is necessary if the fish is served in a sauce. When fish is the principal dish, you might want to serve a vegetable accompaniment. The French favourite is boiled or steamed potatoes, though more and more chefs now add a green vegetable such as courgettes or green beans.

A sauce for fish may be based on the cooking liquid from the fish, or it may be made separately, like Hollandaise for poached fish. Half the pleasure of eating fish in France is the sauce which nearly always accompanies it! Poached or fried fish is usually served with a sauce; baked or stewed fish, on the other hand, is in France often prepared *in* a sauce. An example of this would be the vigorous sauce used for the Baked Sea Bass Niçoise on page 33.

Sole Fillets Normandy-style

Filets de Sole Normande

This dish contains generous amounts of the butter and cream for which Normandy is famous.

1 litre/1¾ pints mussels
3 tablespoons white wine
225 g/8 oz cooked peeled prawns
675 g/1½ lb sole fillets
25 g/1 oz butter
2 shallots, finely chopped
225 g/8 oz button mushrooms, thinly sliced
fish stock (page 20)
2 egg yolks
3 tablespoons single cream
Mushroom Velouté Sauce
reserved fish cooking liquid and mushrooms
strained mussel cooking liquid
40 g/1½ oz butter
3 tablespoons flour

Wash the mussels under running water, scraping with a small knife to remove any seaweed. Discard any broken shells or open shells that do not close when tapped as these are inedible. Place the mussels and white wine in a large non-aluminium saucepan. Cover and cook over high heat, tossing often for 3 to 4 minutes until the shells have opened. Discard any mussels which do not open and remove the mussel meat from the opened shells. Strain the cooking liquid through muslin, then set aside. Halve the prawns lengthwise. Rinse the sole fillets and pat dry with absorbent kitchen paper.

Spread the bottom of a medium-sized frying pan with half the butter. Cut a piece of greaseproof paper to fit the top of the frying pan and butter one side of it. Sprinkle the shallots over the butter in the frying pan and place the mushrooms on top. Fold the fish fillets in half with the skin inside and place narrow side down on the mushrooms. Pour enough stock over the fillets to just cover and season to taste with salt and white pepper. Cover with the greaseproof paper and a lid, if possible. Simmer gently for 7 to 10 minutes until the fish can be flaked easily with a fork. Cool slightly then lift out the fillets and drain on absorbent kitchen paper. Reserve the fish liquid and the mushrooms. Arrange the fillets in a buttered ovenproof serving dish and keep warm.

To make the Mushroom Velouté Sauce place the fish liquid with the mushrooms in a saucepan and boil uncovered until reduced to about 450 ml/¾ pint. Add the mussel liquid. Melt the butter in a heavy saucepan and whisk in the flour. Cook for 1 to 2 minutes until foaming but not browned. Cool slightly, then whisk in the fish liquid and mushrooms. Bring to the boil, whisking constantly. Simmer for 2 minutes or until the sauce is thick enough to coat the back of a spoon.

Whisk the egg yolks and cream in a small bowl and stir in a little hot sauce. Stir the mixture into the remaining sauce. Heat gently and stir until thickened slightly. Do not boil or the sauce will curdle. Remove the sauce from heat and add the remaining butter, cut in small pieces. The cooked fish can be covered and kept warm in a cool oven (150 C, 300 F, gas 2) for up to 15 minutes. The sauce can be kept hot in a water bath (page 16). Just before serving, preheat the grill. Taste the sauce for seasoning and spoon over the fish. Place under the grill until browned. **Serves 6–8 as a starter or 4 as a main course**

Sautéed Fish Steaks

Darnes de Poisson Sautées

Middle cut fish steaks are the best to use for this dish.

4 fish steaks such as salmon, cod, haddock or bass, cut 1.5-cm/¾-in thick
50 g/2 oz butter
salt and pepper
Garnish
slices of lemon
1 tablespoon chopped parsley

Rinse the fish steaks and pat dry with absorbent kitchen paper. Heat the butter in a heavy frying pan over medium heat until foaming. Add the fish steaks and sauté for 2 to 3 minutes until browned. Turn the steaks and sprinkle with salt and pepper. Sauté until the second side is browned and the flesh just flakes easily with a fork. Do not overcook. Place on a warmed serving dish and garnish with slices of lemon and parsley. Serve with Béarnaise or Hollandaise Sauce (pages 74 and 75). **Serves 4**

Fish Croquettes

Croquettes de Poisson

The outside of a croquette, literally a crunchy morsel, should be crisp and the centre creamy.

350 g/12 oz cooked fish, flaked and skin and bones discarded
pinch of cayenne
thick basic white sauce (page 69) made with 250 ml/8 fl oz milk
salt and pepper (optional)
1 egg
2 tablespoons vegetable oil
2 tablespoons water
100 g/4 oz dry white breadcrumbs
½ teaspoon salt
¼ teaspoon pepper
50 g/2 oz plain flour
oil for deep-frying
1 medium-sized bunch parsley, washed and dried

Stir the fish and cayenne into the thick basic white sauce. Taste for seasoning and add salt and pepper if necessary. Spread the mixture on an oiled ice tray or loaf pan, rub the surface with butter and refrigerate for 2 to 3 hours until very firm.

Beat the egg with the oil and water and put the breadcrumbs into a shallow dish. Add ½ teaspoon salt and ¼ teaspoon pepper to the flour and sprinkle it on the work surface. Turn out the chilled croquette mixture and cut into 8 equal pieces. Roll each piece on the floured surface to form cylindrical shapes about 7.5 cm/3 in long and 2.5 cm/1 in. in diameter. Brush each cylinder with the egg mixture and roll in breadcrumbs, making sure that each croquette is completely coated. Chill uncovered on a plate or baking sheet for at least 30 minutes.

Heat the oil for deep-frying to 180 C/350 F and fry the croquettes a few at a time for 2 to 3 minutes until golden brown. Do not overcook or they will burst. Keep hot in a cool oven (150 C, 300 F, gas 2) with the door ajar while frying the remaining croquettes. Allow the oil to cool slightly. Dry the parsley thoroughly and tie the stems in a bunch with string – wet parsley can cause hot fat to bubble and boil over. Lower the parsley into the fat in a basket or on a slotted spoon, standing back as it will splatter. Lift out after 10 seconds or when the splattering stops and drain briefly on absorbent kitchen paper. Cut or break off parsley stems and discard. Sprinkle leafy sprigs over the croquettes. Serve immediately with Béarnaise or Tomato Sauce (pages 73 and 74). **Makes 8 croquettes**

Baked Sea Bass Niçoise

Loup au Four Niçoise

Olives, garlic, olive oil and tomatoes make the cuisine of Nice vigorous and colourful.

4 tablespoons olive oil
2 cloves garlic, crushed
2 teaspoons paprika
3 tablespoons concentrated tomato purée
1 teaspoon dried thyme
salt and pepper
250 ml/8 fl oz white wine or tomato juice
1 (2.25 to 2.75-kg/5 to 6-lb) whole sea bass, scaled and cleaned
50 g/2 oz black olives, stoned
1 lemon, thinly sliced, to garnish

Heat the oven to moderate (180 C, 350 F, gas 4). Heat the oil in a small saucepan. Add the garlic, cook for 1 minute them remove from the heat and stir in the paprika, tomato purée, thyme, salt and pepper to taste and the wine or tomato juice. Simmer for 2 to 3 minutes, then remove from the heat and cool completely.

Grease a large baking dish or roasting tin. Rinse and dry the fish and trim away the fins. Cut the tail to a neat 'V' shape. Place the fish in the prepared baking dish or roasting tin and score with deep diagonal slashes 5 cm/2 in apart. Spoon the sauce over the fish and bake for a further 10 to 15 minutes until the fish can just be flaked easily with a fork. Transfer the fish to a large serving plate or serve from the baking dish. Garnish the fish with overlapping lemon slices. **Serves 4–6**

Variations

Red Mullet Niçoise (*Rouget au Four à la Niçoise*) Substitute red mullet for sea bass.

Cold Fish Niçoise (*Poisson Froid à la Niçoise*) Bake the fish, allow to cool and chill for at least 2 and not more than 8 hours. To serve, transfer to a serving plate and decorate with lemon slices.

Fish Fillets Meunière

Filets de Poisson Meunière

The name refers to the flour coating which seals in the juices.

675 g/1½ lb fish fillets
25 g/1 oz flour
salt and pinch of white pepper
juice of 1 lemon
1 tablespoon chopped parsley
2 teaspoons chopped fresh herbs such as chives, chervil or tarragon
100 g/4 oz butter

Wash the fish fillets then pat dry with absorbent kitchen paper. Mix the flour with ¼ teaspoon salt and a pinch of white pepper. Coat the fillets with flour mixture and shake off the excess. Combine the lemon juice, parsley, other herbs and a pinch of salt and white pepper.

In a large frying pan heat half the butter until foaming; add the fillets. If all the fillets will not fit in one layer, cook in two batches, adding more butter if necessary. Cook over medium heat for 1 to 3 minutes until golden brown; do not overcook or the fish will fall apart. Turn the fillets over and brown the other side. Remove from the pan and keep them warm on a hot serving plate, then wipe the frying pan with absorbent kitchen paper. Add the remaining butter and heat until nut brown. Immediately add the lemon juice mixture, swirling the pan quickly to blend with the butter. Pour the foaming mixture over the fish and serve immediately. **Serves 6–8 as a starter or 4 as a main course**

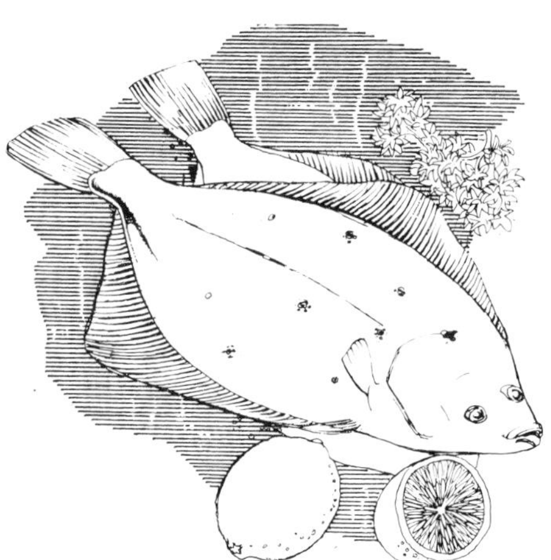

Quenelles with Prawns

Quenelles aux Crevettes

An equally delicious relative of the famous Quenelles Nantua, which require crayfish in the sauce.

choux pastry (page 117) made with 65 g/2½ oz flour
675 g/1½ lb haddock, whiting or cod
3 egg whites, lightly beaten
150 ml/¼ pint whipping cream
salt and pepper
pinch of grated nutmeg

Prawn Sauce

50 g/2 oz butter
½ small onion, finely chopped
1 clove garlic, finely chopped
25 g/1 oz flour
750 ml milk/1¼ pints milk
300 ml/½ pint white veal stock *or* chicken stock (both page 19)
350 g/12 oz raw prawns in the shell
salt and pepper
4 teaspoons brandy
2 tablespoons Tomato Sauce (page 73) *or* 1 teaspoon concentrated tomato purée
4 tablespoons single cream

Prepare the choux pastry, using less egg than called for to get a stiff mixture. Rub the surface with butter while still warm to prevent a skin forming.

Remove any pieces of skin or bone from the fish and purée in a liquidiser or food processor or put through a mincer twice using the fine blade. For a finer texture, work the puréed fish mixture through a fine sieve into a bowl. Refrigerate for 1 hour or until chilled. Place the bowl of fish purée in a pan of iced water and gradually work in the egg whites, beating vigorously with a wooden spoon. Alternatively place the fish in the bowl of a large mixer and whisk in the whites. Gradually beat in the choux pastry mixture followed by the cream. Season to taste with salt, pepper and nutmeg. The salt will slightly thicken the mixture. Use immediately or place in the refrigerator.

Prepare the prawn sauce. Melt the butter in a large frying pan. Add the onion and garlic. Stir constantly over low heat for 5 minutes or until soft but not browned. Stir in the flour and continue to cook, stirring constantly, until foaming but not browned. Add the milk, stock, prawns and salt and pepper to taste. Bring to the boil, reduce the heat and simmer for 5 minutes. Remove the prawns and shell them, reserving the meat. Crush the shells and add these with the brandy to the sauce. Simmer for 10 minutes. Strain the sauce and stir

Quenelles with Prawns

Holding a tablespoon in each hand, press the mixture into egg shapes.

Arrange the poached quenelles in a baking dish and coat with sauce. Garnish with the reserved prawns.

in the tomato sauce or tomato purée and cream. Taste and adjust the seasoning.

Pour water to a depth of 7.5 cm/3 in into a shallow roasting tin or sauté pan and add a generous pinch of salt. Bring to the boil, reduce the heat and simmer gently. Shape one oval quenelle, using 2 tablespoons dipped in the pan of hot water, and drop into the simmering water. Poach for 10 to 15 minutes, depending on size. Remove with a slotted spoon and drain on absorbent kitchen paper.

Heat the oven to moderately hot (190 C, 375 F, gas 5). Arrange the quenelles in buttered individual heatproof dishes or in one large buttered baking dish. Sprinkle with the reserved prawns or use prawns to garnish after coating with sauce. Coat the quenelles generously with sauce and bake for 10 to 15 minutes until the sauce is browned and the quenelles are slightly risen.
Serves 6–8 as a starter or 4 as a main course

Snails with Garlic Butter

Escargots à la Bourguignonne

Serve snail shells in special plates or stand them upright on beds of rock salt.

1 shallot, finely chopped
2 cloves garlic, finely chopped
3 tablespoons chopped parsley
salt and pepper
225 g/8 oz butter, softened
36 snail shells
36 canned snails, thoroughly drained

Preheat the oven to moderate (175 C, 350 F, gas 4). Beat the shallot, garlic, parsley and salt and pepper to taste into the butter. Or combine the shallots, garlic, parsley and butter in a food processor, then add salt and pepper. Spoon $\frac{1}{2}$ teaspoon butter mixture into each snail shell and place a snail on top; cover equally with the remaining butter mixture. Arrange the snail shells in 6 individual snail plates or on rock salt in shallow baking dishes. Bake for 10 minutes or until the butter bubbles. Serve immediately. **Serves 6**

Salmon Mousse

Mousse de Saumon

The rich flavour of salmon is best for this dish, but you can also use cod or smoked haddock.

1 (450-g/1-lb) piece salmon
450 ml/¾ pint fish stock (page 20)
salt and pepper
25 g/1 oz powdered gelatine
3 tablespoons water
2 teaspoons concentrated tomato purée
2 to 3 tablespoons Madeira
pinch of nutmeg
150 ml/¼ pint double cream
1 small cucumber to garnish
hot toast for serving

Rinse and dry the salmon. Place in a medium saucepan and pour over the fish stock. Sprinkle with salt and pepper. Bring to the boil and poach over low heat for 12 to 15 minutes until the flesh just flakes easily with a fork. Allow to cool in the cooking liquid then drain, reserving the liquid in a saucepan. Discard the skin and bones and flake the fish. Soak the gelatine in 3 tablespoons water to soften. Bring the cooking liquid to a boil, remove from the heat, add the softened gelatine and stir until completely dissolved. Cool completely.

In a liquidiser or food processor, blend the salmon with the gelatine mixture. Turn the mixture into a large bowl and stir in the tomato purée, Madeira, nutmeg, salt and pepper. Place the bowl in a larger bowl of iced water. Rinse a 1.15-litre/2-pint charlotte mould or other metal mould with water. Stir the salmon mixture until cold and on the point of setting. Whip the cream lightly then fold into the salmon mixture. Taste for seasoning and spoon into the mould. Cover and chill for at least 2 hours or until firmly set. Salmon Mousse can be made 2 days ahead and refrigerated, but serve it at room temperature.

Turn out the mousse not more than 4 hours before serving. To unmould, carefully run a knife around the edges and dip the bottom of the mould in a pan of lukewarm water for a few seconds. Unmould on to a serving plate. Use a vegetable peeler to remove alternate strips of peel from cucumber then cut the cucumber into thin slices. Garnish the mousse with slices of cucumber. Serve with hot toast. **Serves 8–10**

Scallops Parisienne

Coquilles St Jacques Parisienne

For economy, replace some of the scallops with white fish fillets poached for 7 minutes and cubed.

450 g/1 lb fresh or thawed frozen scallops
450 ml/¾ pint fish stock (page 20)
pinch of salt
175 g/6 oz mushrooms, quartered
juice of ½ lemon
salt and pepper
1 quantity duchess potatoes (page 84)
40 g/1½ oz butter
1 onion, finely chopped
2 tablespoons flour
6 tablespoons single cream
25 g/1 oz dry breadcrumbs
2 to 3 tablespoons melted butter

Rinse and drain the scallops. Put the stock in a large shallow saucepan and add the scallops and a pinch of salt. Cover and poach small scallops for 1 to 2 minutes or large scallops for 2 to 3 minutes until no longer transparent in the centre. Do not overcook or they will become tough. Cool slightly and drain, reserving the cooking liquid. Discard the small membrane on the side of each scallop. Cut large scallops into 2 or 3 diagonal slices. In a medium saucepan, put mushrooms, lemon juice and salt and pepper to taste into a 5-cm/¼-in depth of water. Cover tightly and cook over a high heat for 3 to 5 minutes until the liquid boils to the top of the pan and the mushrooms are tender. Drain, reserving the liquid.

Preheat the oven to moderately hot (200 C, 400 F, gas 6). Butter 4 to 6 deep scallop shells, or individual ovenproof dishes. Using a piping bag with a medium star tube pipe a border of duchess potatoes around the edges of each dish. Melt 40 g/1½ oz butter in a medium-sized saucepan. Add the onion and cook until soft but not brown. Whisk in the flour and cook until foaming. Cool slightly and whisk in the reserved cooking liquid from the scallops and mushrooms. Bring the sauce to the boil, whisking all the time, and simmer for 2 minutes. Add the cream and if necessary boil for a further few minutes until the sauce is thick enough to coat the back of a spoon. Taste and adjust the seasoning then stir in the mushrooms and scallops. Taste again and spoon into prepared shells or dishes. Sprinkle with breadcrumbs and melted butter. Bake for 10 to 15 minutes or until bubbling and browned. **Serves 6 as a starter or 4 as a main course**

Scampi Newburg

Langoustines à la Newburg

Heat the scampi and sauce in a chafing dish at the table.

Rice Pilaf (page 85)
100 g/4 oz butter
675 g/$1\frac{1}{2}$ lb cooked, peeled scampi or large prawns
$\frac{1}{2}$ teaspoon paprika
salt and pepper
450 ml/$\frac{3}{4}$ pint single cream
6 egg yolks
4 tablespoons brandy

Prepare the Rice Pilaff according to the recipe instructions. Grease a 900-ml/$1\frac{1}{2}$-pint ring mould and fill with the rice, pressing lightly. Keep warm and turn out onto a round serving plate just before preparing the scampi mixture.

Spread 40 g/$1\frac{1}{2}$ oz of the butter in a shallow saucepan or chafing dish. Add the scampi or prawns and sprinkle with paprika, salt and pepper. Cover and heat gently for 2 to 3 minutes. Whisk the cream and egg yolks in a small bowl until blended. Add the brandy to the scampi mixture and flame. Remove from the heat and stir in the cream mixture. Heat gently, stirring constantly, until the sauce thickens. Do not overheat or the mixture will curdle. Remove the pan from the heat and add the remaining butter cut in small pieces, shaking the pan until the butter mixes into the sauce. Taste and adjust the seasoning. Spoon the scampi into the rice ring with a little sauce. Serve at once with the remaining sauce served separately. **Serves 4**

Variation

Lobster Newburg (*Homard à la Newburg*) Substitute 675 g/$1\frac{1}{2}$ lb cooked lobster meat for the scampi.

Crab Gratin

Gratin de Crabe

This dish is also delicious made with cooked lobster or prawns.

4 large cooked crabs or 675 g/$1\frac{1}{2}$ lb crab meat
25 g/1 oz butter
4 shallots, finely chopped
250 ml/8 fl oz white wine
thick basic white sauce (page 69) made with 900 ml/$1\frac{1}{2}$ pints milk
2 teaspoons powdered mustard
3 tablespoons French mustard
1 teaspoon brandy
150 ml/$\frac{1}{4}$ pint single cream
salt and pepper (optional)
2 oz Gruyère cheese, grated

If using whole crabs, remove the meat from the claws and body, being careful to discard all pieces of membrane. Reserve any coral. There should be about 675 g/$1\frac{1}{2}$ lb crabmeat. Heat the oven to moderately hot (200 C, 400 F, gas 6). Melt the butter in a medium saucepan and use to sauté the shallots over a low heat for 2 to 3 minutes. Add the wine and boil untlil reduced to about 4 tablespoons. Stir this mixture into the thick basic white sauce with the two kinds of mustard. Stir in the brandy and cream and warm gently over low heat. Stir in the crabmeat and coral then taste and adjust the seasoning. Spoon the mixture into the crab shells or a buttered shallow baking dish and rub with butter to prevent a skin forming. Sprinkle with the grated cheese and bake for 10 to 15 minutes until bubbling and browned.
Serves 6 as a main course or 10 as a starter

Trout in Paper Parcels

Truites en Papillote

Greaseproof paper is preferable to foil because it puffs up and browns attractively in the oven.

4 whole trout, cleaned
100 g/4 oz butter
salt and pepper
DUXELLES
25 g/1 oz butter
1 shallot, finely chopped
225 g/8 oz mushrooms, finely chopped
2 tablespoons chopped parsley
salt and pepper

Preheat the oven to moderate (175 C, 350 F, gas 4). Rinse and dry the fish. To prepare the duxelles: melt the butter in a medium-sized frying pan and use to sauté the shallot over a low heat for 2 to 3 minutes until soft but not browned. Add the mushrooms and stir constantly over high heat until all the moisture has evaporated. Remove from the heat, stir in the parsley and season with salt and pepper. Cut 4 large heart shapes out of greaseproof paper or foil large enough to enclose each fish, leaving a 5-cm/2-in border. Spread the centre of each paper with a small knob of butter and place the fish on the butter. Sprinkle the fish inside and out with salt and pepper and fill the inside with the duxelles. Fold the paper over the fish, turn over the paper edges and pleat to seal. The trout can be prepared to this point 3 to 4 hours ahead and chilled, but the duxelles must be cold before being put into the fish.

Place the parcels on a baking sheet and bake for 15 to 18 minutes until the parcels have puffed up. Warm the remaining butter in a water bath or over very low heat, stirring constantly; the butter should soften but not melt and become oily. Serve the fish parcels at once on warmed plates so that they do not have time to cool and deflate. Cut open before serving or let guests open their own. Serve softened butter separately. **Serves 4**

Trout in Paper Parcels

Pleat edges of the greaseproof paper or foil to seal well.

Cut the paper with a sharp knife before serving at the table.

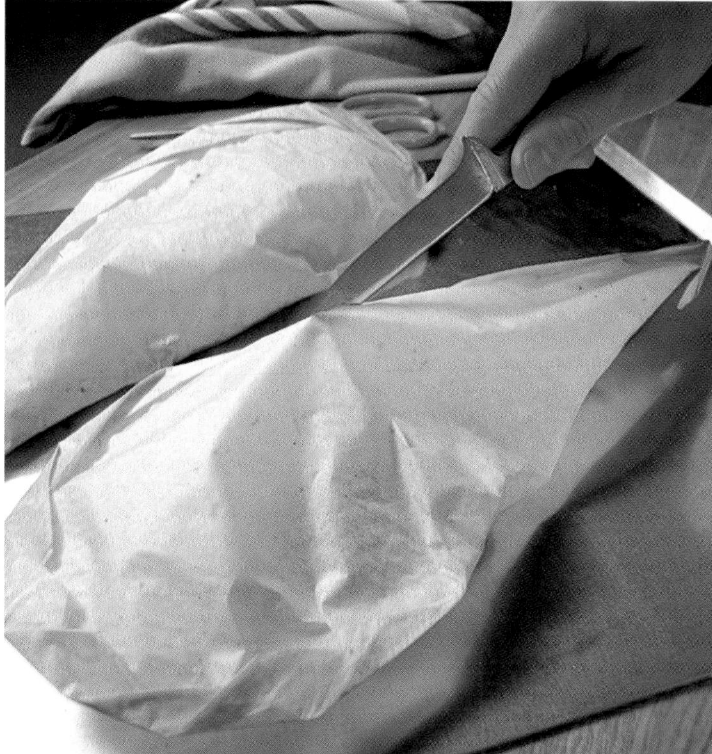

Poultry

From simple family meals to festive dinners, poultry can form the main part of almost any menu. Poultry of one kind or another goes with virtually every sauce, vegetable and even fruit.

Birds are generally divided into two categories: those with white flesh and little natural fat and those with dark, rich meat and fatty skin. Chicken is the most familiar in the first group, and duck is outstanding in the second.

Of all birds, chicken is the most versatile. It can be grilled, roasted, poached, braised – indeed, cooked in almost any way. And chicken is as much at home with the delicate wine and cream sauces of the Loire Valley as with the robust garnish of bacon, potatoes, olives, tomatoes and mushrooms from Corsica.

For this reason you can change ingredients in chicken dishes almost at will, substituting red wine for white and strips of courgettes for green beans. You can add or omit mushrooms, onions, garlic, bacon, tomatoes, herbs or cream as it suits you.

Duck is a different matter. It is usually roasted to dissolve its fat and give a crisp skin. Because of its meaty flesh, duck is good with brown sauces, fortified wines such as Madeira and sherry, and with fruit or sharp flavours to complement its richness.

Turkey is the natural choice for serving large numbers and is usually stuffed to provide extra portions as well as extra flavour. Mixtures are usually based on meat or on cereals.

How to Choose and Cook Poultry

When buying poultry, try to choose plump chickens; a thin, bony chicken, no matter how well cooked, looks sad on the platter. Try to find ducks that are not too fat; French ducks are relatively lean. Small turkeys are usually more moist than very large ones.

The aim in cooking poultry is to keep it moist. If cooked too long, a bird dries out, but if undercooked, it will be tough. One way to help retain juices is to cook a bird whole. Roast chicken is as much of a favourite in France as it is in the rest of the world. All except the largest birds are roasted at relatively high heat to ensure a crisp skin. Constant basting, especially during roasting of white-fleshed birds, is needed to keep poultry moist. A related French method which saves time and effort is pot roasting *en cocotte*. The bird is browned all over in melted butter and then cooked in the oven in a covered casserole, often together with the garnish. Little or no liquid is needed.

Like fish and meat, chicken can be cooked in liquid, which both gives and receives flavour. Poaching, preferably in stock made beforehand with some chicken bones, is an efficient way to keep birds particularly moist. For this reason, it is the preferred method of cooking a chicken which will be served cold. When poultry is cut in pieces, it is usually browned in fat first, then simmered in liquid from which is made a richly flavoured sauce, as in the famous Coq au Vin.

Getting Ahead

Poultry cooked in sauce reheats very well, so it can be refrigerated for a day or two, or frozen. However, roasted or pot-roasted birds lose their fresh taste and crisp skin when reheated. If there is any left over it is much better to serve it cold. Serve cold chicken or turkey with mayonnaise and duck with pickles, citrus or spicy poached fruit or green salad.

How to Check if Poultry is Done

For whole birds pierce the body with a two-pronged fork and, if the bird is small enough, lift it up and tip the juices from inside. Note the colour of the juices that escape. A white-fleshed bird is done when the juice is no longer pink but clear. A duck is done French-style when the juice is no longer red but light pink. However, many people prefer their duck well done, in which case the juice should be clear.

For cut birds, stuffed birds and those too heavy to lift, gently prick the thickest part of the leg with a two-pronged fork and note the colour of the juices. Do not test too often or the bird will lose a good deal of juice.

Chicken in Wine

Coq au Vin

Coq au Vin *is a traditional dish, originally designed to tenderise a tough old chicken. It is now widely made throughout France.*

1 (1.5-kg/3½-lb) oven-ready roasting chicken cut into 8 pieces
1 tablespoon vegetable oil
15 g/½ oz butter
100 g/4 oz streaky bacon
20 pickling onions, peeled
225 g/8 oz mushrooms, quartered
15 g/½ oz plain flour
450 ml/¾ pint chicken stock (page 19)
1 clove garlic, finely chopped
2 shallots, finely chopped
1 bouquet garni
salt and pepper
1 tablespoon chopped parsley

MARINADE

450 ml/¾ pint red wine
1 onion, thinly sliced
1 carrot, thinly sliced
1 bouquet garni
1 clove garlic, sliced
6 peppercorns
2 tablespoons olive oil

Mix all the ingredients for the marinade together and pour over the chicken pieces in a deep bowl. Leave to marinate for 6 hours at room temperature or 10 to 12 hours in the refrigerator, turning the chicken pieces occasionally.

Drain the chicken, reserving the marinade, and pat dry with absorbent kitchen paper. Strain the marinade, discarding vegetables and seasonings. Heat the oil and butter in a frying pan or flameproof casserole and fry the bacon until browned; remove from the pan. Sauté the onions until lightly browned and remove from the pan. Then fry the mushrooms until tender and remove from the pan. Place the chicken pieces in the pan skin side down and brown both sides thoroughly over medium heat for 5 to 10 minutes. Remove from the pan. Discard all but 2 tablespoons fat, stir in the flour and cook until foaming. Add the reserved liquid from the marinade then add the garlic, shallots, bouquet garni and a little salt and pepper. Return the chicken to the pan, cover and bring to the boil. Reduce the heat and simmer for 20–30 minutes until chicken is almost tender, stirring occasionally to prevent sticking. Stir in the onions and simmer for a further 10 minutes. Place the chicken on a serving plate and cover with foil to keep warm. Discard the bouquet garni. Stir the mushrooms and bacon into the sauce and if necessary boil the sauce until thick enough to coat the back of a spoon. Taste and adjust the seasoning. Spoon the sauce over the chicken. Sprinkle with parsley before serving. **Serves 4**

Roast Chicken Fermière

Poulet Rôti à la Fermière

Almost any young spring vegetables can be added to this dish.

1 (1.5-kg/3½-lb) oven-ready roasting chicken, trussed
15 g/½ oz butter
2 tablespoons vegetable oil
salt and pepper
450 g/1 lb potatoes
100 g/4 oz bacon, diced
20 pickling onions, peeled
225 g/8 oz button mushrooms

Preheat the oven to moderately hot (200 C, 400 F, gas 6). Rub the chicken with the butter. Pour the oil into a roasting tin. Place the chicken on one side in the pan and sprinkle with salt and pepper. Roast in the oven for 15 minutes, basting occasionally. Peel and quarter the potatoes. Turn the chicken onto the other side. Arrange the potatoes round the chicken and sprinkle with salt and pepper. Roast for a further 15 minutes, basting frequently. Meanwhile dry fry the bacon in a heavy frying pan until browned; remove and reserve. Cook the onions in the same pan, shaking from time to time to make sure the onions are browned on all sides. Remove and reserve them, then quickly brown the mushrooms in the same way. Place the chicken on its back breast side up and add the bacon, onions and mushrooms to the roasting tin. Roast for a further 10 to 20 minutes until the skin is crisp and browned and the juices run clear. Transfer the chicken to a warmed serving plate and discard any trussing strings. Spoon the vegetables and bacon around the chicken before serving. **Serves 4**

Page 16

MORAY FIRTH STUFFED TROUT

(Serves 4)

4 Medium Trout
1 Small onion — finely chopped
4 ozs Watercress, chopped
2 ozs Mixed nuts, chopped
4 ozs Prawns
2 ozs Fresh wholemeal breadcrumbs
1 Beaten egg
1 oz melted butter

Method

1. Remove heads from trout, remove the back bone.
2. Melt the butter and saute the onion until soft, or microwave this for 2 mins.
3. Combine together the onion, cress, breadcrumbs, nuts, prawns and bind together with beaten egg.
4. Lightly grease a shallow ovenproof dish. Stuff the trout and brush with a little melted butter. Place the trout side by side into oven dish
5. Cover and bake in a moderate oven for about 20 mins. or microwave for 6-8 minutes. garnish with slices of lemon and serve with a mixed green salad.

This is a truly delicious Supper or Dinner Party dish. Quick and easy to make.

Pot-Roast
cken

otte à la Corsoise

Mediterranean colour to this
en dish.

is vegetable oil
oz butter
n cut into large dice
ready roasting chicken
d pepper
ized potatoes
s, drained and stoned
on mushrooms
halved and deseeded
of garlic
ons brandy
pped parsley (optional)

tely hot (200 C, 400 F, gas 6).
l and 15 g/$\frac{1}{2}$ oz of the butter
role. Add the gammon and
until browned and crisp.
the chicken to the casserole
prinkle lightly with salt and
k in the oven for 20 minutes.
es then place them in a small
ld water. Bring the water to
tatoes at once. Heat the re-
ether in a frying pan and use
ickly on all sides. Sprinkle
. Remove from the heat and
ushrooms, tomatoes, garlic
Cover tightly and cook for
chicken is tender. Taste the
the seasoning. Discard any
chicken and arrange in a
over the vegetable garnish
inkle with parsley. **Serves 4**

Chicken Kiev

Poulet à la Kiev

A pocket of herb butter is hidden in each deep-fried chicken breast.

75 g/3 oz butter
grated rind and juice of 1 lemon
1 tablespoon finely chopped parsley
1 tablespoon finely chopped tarragon or 1 teaspoon dried tarragon
1 teaspoon finely chopped chives
salt and pepper
4 boneless chicken breasts
25 g/1 oz plain flour
1 egg
1 tablespoon vegetable oil
1 tablespoon water
100 g/4 oz dry white breadcrumbs
oil for deep frying

Cream the butter in a small bowl. Beat in the lemon rind and juice, parsley, tarragon, chives and plenty of salt and pepper. Shape into a 7.5-cm/3-in square cake and place on a sheet of greaseproof paper. Cover and put in the freezer or refrigerator until very firm. Remove the skin from the chicken breasts and place on a flat work surface. With the tip of a sharp knife cut a deep slit in the thick edge of each chicken breast to make a pocket, taking care not to cut through the opposite side of the breast. Cut the chilled herb butter into four sticks and slip one stick into each pocket. Press the edges of the pocket together with your fingertips, making sure that no butter is visible. Mix the flour with $\frac{1}{4}$ teaspoon salt and a pinch of pepper on a plate. In a wide shallow bowl beat the egg with the oil and water. Roll the chicken breasts in seasoned flour, dip both sides in the beaten egg mixture and coat thoroughly with breadcrumbs. Chill the coated chicken pieces for 2–3 hours or overnight so that the bread coating will dry out and be very crisp when fried.

Heat the oil for deep frying to 180 C/350 F and fry the breasts two at a time until golden brown – about 5 minutes. Drain on absorbent kitchen paper and serve immediately. Chicken Kiev can be kept hot for 5 to 10 minutes in a cool oven (120 C, 250 F, gas $\frac{1}{2}$). **Serves 4**

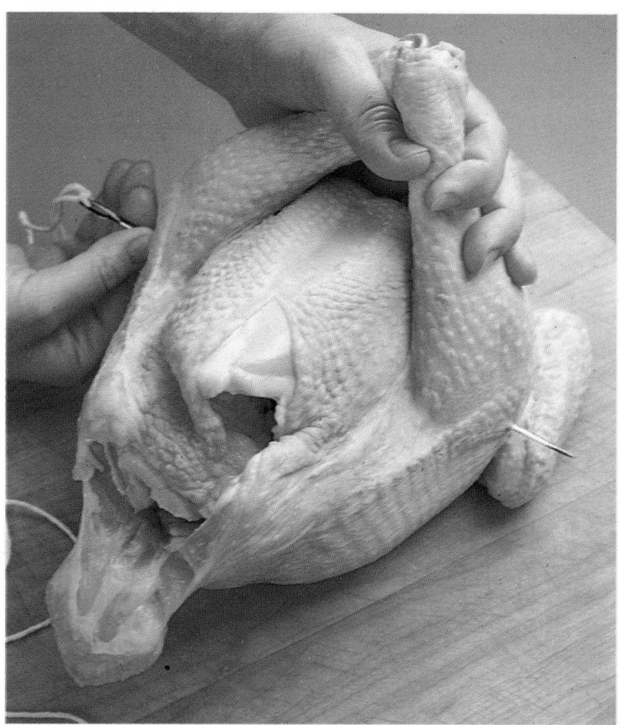

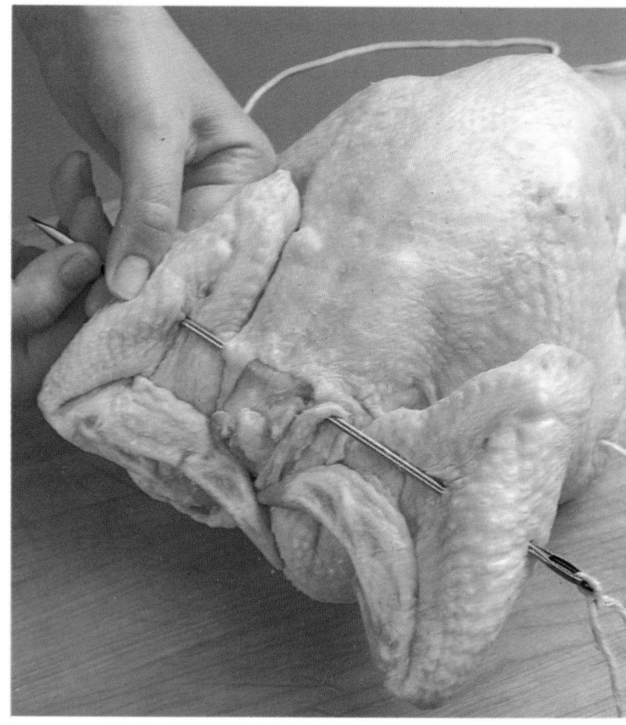

Chicken with Tarragon

Poulet à l'Estragon

If fresh tarragon is not available, use fresh rosemary, oregano, dill or parsley.

1 (1.5-kg/3½-lb) oven-ready roasting chicken, trussed, with giblets reserved
salt and pepper
40 g/1½ oz bunch fresh tarragon
75 g/3 oz butter
1 onion, coarsely chopped,
1 carrot, diced
450 ml to 1.25 litres/2 to 3 pints chicken stock (page 19)
1 bouquet garni
20 g/¾ oz plain flour
4 tablespoons double cream
Rice Pilaf (page 85) to serve

Sprinkle the cavity of the chicken generously with salt and pepper. Strip the leaves from half the tarragon stems, reserve the leaves and place the stems inside the cavity of the chicken. Truss the chicken following the instructions on page 43. Melt half the butter in a large flameproof casserole and brown the chicken on all sides over a medium heat. Stir in the onion, carrot and reserved giblets except for the liver and cook until lightly browned. Add enough stock to come three-quarters of the way up the chicken. Reserve and chill 3 tablespoons of the stock. Add the bouquet garni, the stems from the remaining tarragon and a little salt and pepper to the casserole. Cover and bring to the boil. Reduce the heat and simmer for 45 to 50 minutes or until the juices run clear.

Transfer the chicken to a plate, remove the trussing strings, cover with foil and keep warm. Skim excess fat from the cooking liquid and reduce by rapid boiling to about 600 ml/1 pint. Taste and adjust the seasoning, then strain. Fill a small saucepan two-thirds full of water and bring to the boil. Add the tarragon leaves and blanch by boiling for 1 minute. Drain and refresh with cold water. Mix the flour and reserved cold stock in a cup to make a smooth paste. Gradually whisk the paste into the boiling broth and continue whisking until it thickens enough to coat the back of a spoon. Stir in the cream and bring back just to the boil. Add half the blanched tarragon leaves. Taste for seasoning.

If carving the chicken at the table, spoon a little sauce over the whole chicken and sprinkle with the remaining blanched tarragon leaves. Serve with the Rice Pilaf piled around the chicken. Alternatively, carve the chicken into 8 pieces and arrange on one side of the serving dish. Coat them with sauce and decorate with the remaining blanched tarragon leaves. Spoon the Rice Pilaf on to the other side of plate. In either case hand the remaining sauce separately. **Serves 4–6**

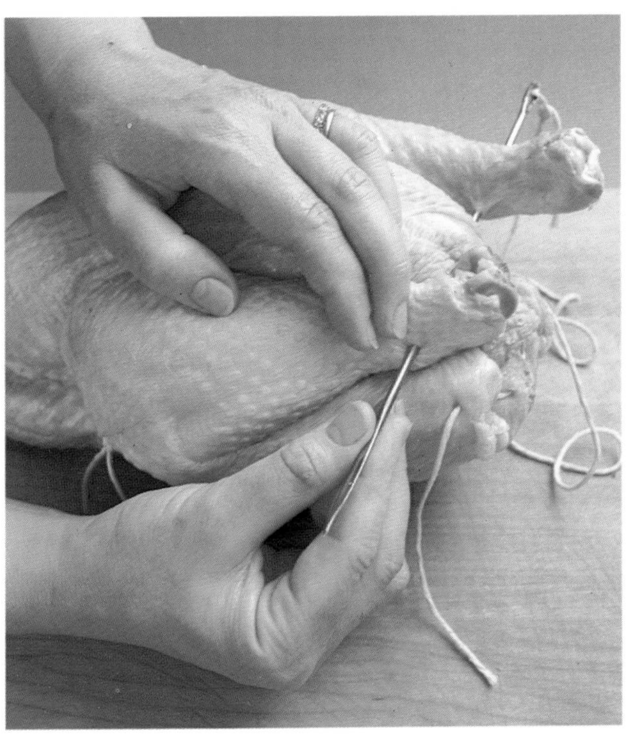

Trussing a chicken

Far left Insert a trussing needle through leg at the joint. Push needle through the chicken and out the other side.

Centre Insert the needle into the wing, making a long stitch from leg to wing. Push needle through neck skin, under backbone and through other wing. Cut and tie string.

Left If the chicken is stuffed or large, push threaded needle through the tail, then through drumsticks. Tie tightly.

Anjou Chicken Sauté

Sauté de Poulet à l'Angevine

A rich chicken dish, traditionally made with white wine from Anjou in the Loire Valley.

1 tablespoon vegetable oil
25 g/1 oz butter
1 (1.5-kg/$3\frac{1}{2}$-lb) oven-ready roasting chicken cut into 8 pieces
20 pickling onions, peeled
2 shallots, chopped
150 ml/$\frac{1}{4}$ pint white wine
salt and pepper
225 g/8 oz mushrooms, quartered
150 ml/$\frac{1}{4}$ pint single cream
1 teaspoon arrowroot
1 tablespoon water
1 tablespoon chopped parsley to garnish

Heat the oil and butter in a large frying pan with a lid or flameproof casserole. Brown the chicken pieces on both sides, then remove from the pan. Add the pickling onions to the pan and sauté, shaking the pan so that they brown evenly. Remove from the pan. Stir in the shallots and sauté until soft but not browned. Remove from the pan. Return the chicken pieces to the pan, and add 4 tablespoons of the wine and salt and pepper to taste. Cover tightly and cook over low heat for 35 to 45 minutes until the breast and wings are tender. Remove the breast and wing pieces and keep warm. Add the mushrooms, sautéed onions and shallots and cook with the remaining chicken for a further 10 minutes or until very tender.

Arrange the chicken on a serving dish with the onions and mushrooms and cover with foil to keep warm. Stir the remaining wine into the sauce and bring to the boil. Continue to boil for 2 to 3 minutes, stir in the cream and bring just back to boiling point. Blend the arrowroot and water in a cup to make a paste and gradually whisk this paste into the boiling sauce. Simmer, whisking all the time until the sauce thickens enough to coat the back of a spoon. Taste and adjust the seasoning. Spoon the sauce over the chicken and sprinkle with chopped parsley before serving. **Serves 4**

Chicken Bouchées

Bouchée à la Reine

These delicious 'mouthfuls', as 'bouchée' literally means, are indeed fit for a queen.

puff pastry (page 115) made with 300 g/11 oz butter
beaten egg to glaze
1 (1.5-kg/3½-lb) oven-ready roasting chicken, giblets removed and trussed (page 43)
1 onion, halved
1 carrot, halved
bouquet garni
6 peppercorns
1.2 to 1.4 litres/2 to 2½ pints white veal stock *or* chicken stock (page 18) *or* water
225 g/8 oz mushrooms, quartered
juice of ½ lemon
salt and pepper
50 g/2 oz butter
25 g/1 oz plain flour
3 egg yolks
150 ml/¼ pint single cream

First make the bouchées. Prepare the puff pastry, completing all 6 turns, and chill for at least 1 hour. Preheat the oven to hot (220 C, 425 F, gas 7). Sprinkle water on a baking sheet. Roll out the dough until it is about 5 mm/¼ in thick. Cut out 16 (8.5-cm/3½-in) rounds with a fluted cutter. Place half the rounds on a prepared baking sheet and brush with beaten egg to glaze. Use a plain 6-cm/2½-in cutter to cut a circle from the centre of each remaining round to form rings. Place the rings on top of the glazed rounds and press gently to seal. Chill for 15 minutes. Brush with the egg glaze. Bake for 15 to 20 minutes until risen and golden brown. Transfer to a wire rack to cool. While the bouchées are still warm, remove and reserve the centre 'hat' that has formed. Scoop out any uncooked dough with a teaspoon.

Place the chicken in a heavy casserole with the onion, carrot, bouquet garni, peppercorns and enough stock or water to just cover. Cover and slowly bring to the boil. Reduce the heat and simmer for 1 to 1½ hours or until the juice runs clear. Turn the chicken at least once during cooking. Cool the chicken to lukewarm in the liquid. Drain the cooled chicken, reserving the liquid which should be simmered until reduced to about 750 ml/1¼ pints. Remove the chicken meat from the bones and cut into 1-cm/½-in dice, discarding the skin. In a small saucepan, containing water 5 mm/¼ in deep, put the mushrooms, lemon juice, salt and pepper. Cover and cook over high heat for 4 to 5 minutes until the mushrooms are tender. Drain, reserving the liquid.

Melt the butter in a medium-sized saucepan and whisk in the flour. Cook over a medium heat for 1–2 minutes until foaming but not browned. Cool slightly, then whisk in the reduced stock and mushroom cooking liquid. Bring to the boil, whisking constantly. Continue whisking and simmer for 2 minutes or until the mixture will thickly coat the back of a spoon. Stir in the diced chicken and mushrooms. Taste and adjust the seasoning.

To serve, reheat the bouchées for a few minutes in a very cool oven (120 C, 250 F, gas ½). If necessary, reheat the chicken filling over a medium heat. Beat the egg yolks and cream together in a small bowl and stir in a few tablespoons of the hot filling. Add this mixture to the remaining filling and mix thoroughly. Stir over low heat until the mixture thickens slightly. The sauce should be fairly thick so it doesn't soak the bouchées. Do not boil or it will curdle. Taste and adjust the seasoning, fill each bouchée generously with filling and top with a reserved pastry 'hat'. Serve immediately. **Makes 8**

Turkey with Chestnuts

Dinde aux Marrons

Traditional Christmas turkey in France is stuffed with chestnuts. The same stuffing is also good with chicken.

675 g/1½ lb fresh chestnuts or 1 (1-kg/2-lb) can whole unsweetened chestnuts
1.15 to 1.4 litres/2 to 2½ pints chicken stock or turkey stock (page 19)
salt and pepper
75 g/3 oz butter
2 onions, chopped
675 g/1½ lb pork sausagemeat
3 tablespoons brandy
1 teaspoon allspice
¼ teaspoon nutmeg
1 (2.75 to 3.5-kg/6 to 8-lb) turkey
300 ml/½ pint white wine
1 bunch watercress

If using fresh chestnuts, pierce the tops with a pointed knife and place in a saucepan. Cover with cold water, bring to the boil and remove immediately from the heat. Lift a few at a time out of the water and peel. If the chestnuts cool and become difficult to peel, reheat quickly; but don't cook the chestnuts or they will be impossible to peel. Place the peeled fresh chestnuts in a saucepan with 600 ml/1 pint stock and a little salt and pepper. Cover and simmer for 20 to 30 minutes until tender. Cool to lukewarm and drain. If using canned chestnuts, drain.

Melt 25 g/1 oz of the butter in a frying pan. Stir in the onions and cook until soft but not browned. Add the sausagemeat and cook until brown, stirring to break up the meat. Stir in the brandy, allspice, nutmeg and salt and pepper to taste and continue to cook for a further 2 minutes to blend the flavours. Remove from the heat and gently stir in the chestnuts, taking care not to break them. Allow the stuffing to cool completely. Preheat the oven to moderate (180 C, 350 F, gas 4). Stuff the turkey and truss (page 43). The turkey can be stuffed with chilled stuffing 3 to 4 hours ahead and refrigerated. Spread the breast and legs of the turkey with the remaining butter and sprinkle with salt and pepper. Place the turkey on its side in a roasting tin and pour 300 ml/½ pint stock into the tin. Loosely cover the bird with foil and roast for 3 to 3½ hours until the juice runs clear. During cooking, turn the turkey from one side to the other and then onto its back, basting frequently. If the pan gets dry add more stock. Remove the foil during the last ½ hour of the cooking time so the turkey browns well and the skin becomes crisp.

Transfer the turkey to a serving plate, cover with foil and keep warm. Stir the wine and remaining stock into the roasting tin. Bring to the boil, stirring to dissolve any brown juices on the bottom of the pan. Reduce the gravy until the flavour is concentrated, then season to taste and strain. Remove the trussing strings from the turkey, spoon a little gravy over the bird and serve the rest separately. Garnish with watercress. **Serves 8**

Duck Sauté with Madeira

Sauté de Canard au Madère

1 tablespoon vegetable oil
1 (1.75 to 2.25-kg/4 to 5-lb) duck, quartered
1 onion, chopped
1½ tablespoons plain flour
150 ml/¼ pint red wine
150 ml/¼ pint brown beef stock (page 18) *or* chicken stock (page 19)
1 bouquet garni
2 shallots, chopped
1 clove garlic, crushed
salt and pepper
100 g/4 oz mushrooms, thinly sliced
3 tablespoons Madeira
croûtes (page 22)
1 tablespoon chopped parsley to garnish

Heat the oil in a large frying pan and use to sauté the duck pieces cut side down for 1 to 2 minutes to seal in the juices. Turn over and cook, skin side down, for 15–20 minutes until the pieces are browned and the fat has been rendered so that the duck will not be greasy.

Remove the duck and discard all but 2 tablespoons fat. Stir in the onion and sauté until lightly browned. Add the flour and cook, stirring, over medium heat until browned. Immediately whisk in the wine, stock, bouquet garni, shallots, garlic, salt and pepper. Return the duck to the pan, cover and simmer for 20–30 minutes until tender when pierced with a skewer, adding more stock if the sauce becomes thick.

Add the mushrooms and Madeira and simmer for 2 to 3 minutes until the mushrooms are tender. The sauce should be just thick enough to coat the back of a spoon. If it is too thick, add a little extra stock and if it is too thin, simmer to reduce further. Discard the bouquet garni and taste and adjust the seasoning. Arrange the duck pieces and the croûtes on a serving plate and spoon the mushrooms and sauce over the duck. Sprinkle with parsley just before serving. **Serves 4**

Roast Duck with Orange Sauce

Canard à l'Orange

Boiling the orange peel softens it and reduces its bitterness.

3 oranges
1 (1.75 to 2.25-kg/4 to 5-lb) duck
salt and pepper
3 tablespoons brandy
150 ml/¼ pint white veal stock *or* chicken stock (both page 18)
1 tablespoon Grand Marnier
ORANGE SAUCE
thinly pared rind of 2 of the oranges
150 g/2 oz granulated sugar
3 tablespoons water
3 tablespoons vinegar
neck and gizzard from the duck
2 tablespoons vegetable oil
1 onion, diced
1 carrot, diced
2 tablespoons plain flour
600 ml/1 pint white veal stock (page 18) *or* chicken stock (page 19)

Preheat the oven to moderately hot (200 C, 400 F, gas 6). Use a vegetable peeler to pare the rind from two of the oranges and place a few strips of peel inside the duck, reserving the remaining peel for the sauce. Truss the duck (page 43). Place the duck on one thigh in a roasting tin and sprinkle with salt and pepper. Prick all over to release the fat during cooking. Roast the duck on one side for 20 minutes, then turn over on to the other thigh and cook for a further 20 minutes. Place the duck on its back for the remaining cooking time. Spoon excess fat from the roasting pan occasionally. Continue to roast until the skin is crisp and browned and the juice runs clear. Total cooking time should be 1½–2 hours.

Use a serrated knife to cut the pith from two of the peeled oranges. Separate the segments, discarding the membrane and reserving any juice. Put the orange segments in a small pan with 2 tablespoons of the brandy. Flute the remaining orange by using a canelle knife to cut lengthways grooves and thinly slice for garnish.

Place the cooked duck on a serving plate and remove the trussing string. Cover the duck with foil to keep warm. Discard the fat from the roasting pan and pour in the stock. Bring to the boil, stirring to dissolve any brown juices on the bottom of the pan and strain into the orange sauce with the juice from the orange segments. Add the remaining brandy and Grand Marnier. Heat through gently without boiling. Taste and adjust the seasoning. Stir in the orange segments, spoon a little sauce over the duck and arrange the orange segments on the platter. Garnish with the fluted orange slices and serve with the remaining sauce handed separately. **Serves 3–4**

Orange Sauce

Cut the reserved orange peel into very thin strips and place in a small saucepan two-thirds full of cold water, bring to the boil and boil for 3 to 4 minutes to blanch. Drain, rinse in cold water and drain again; set aside. In a small heavy saucepan, heat the sugar in 3 tablespoons of water until dissolved, then bring to a boil. Continue to boil until the liquid turns to a light brown then remove from the heat immediately. Pour in the vinegar, standing well back as the vinegar vapour can sting the eyes. Heat gently until the caramel is dissolved.

Cut the neck and gizzard of the duck into chunks. Heat the oil in a medium-sized heavy saucepan and sauté the giblet chunks in oil until well browned. Remove from the pan and stir in the diced onion and carrot. Cook over low heat until just beginning to brown, then stir in the flour. Cook, stirring, until browned but do not let the flour scorch. Pour in the stock and bring to the boil, stirring often. Add the browned giblets with the caramel mixture. Simmer for 40–50 minutes stirring occasionally until the sauce is thick enough to coat the back of a spoon and is reduced to 450 ml/¾ pint. Skim the sauce and strain, pressing the vegetables to extract as much liquid as possible. Taste and adjust the seasoning. Stir in the strips of orange peel.

Roast Duck with Orange Sauce (above).

Meat

The French enjoy all types of meat and meat cookery. Although they love juicy roasts and steaks, they have equal regard for more humble casseroles and stews.

How to Choose and Store Meat

When shopping for meat there is much that can be told from appearance. Good beef should have a generous marbling of fat, and if you prefer the mature flavour of well-hung beef look for bright red flesh tinged with purple. Lamb, pork and veal are best when clear and light coloured, a sign that the animal is young. Lamb should be deep pink, pork a pinkish beige and veal a delicate rose. When tinged with red, veal is on its way to becoming beef and, being both insipid and tough, combines the worst of both meats.

Meat should be stored, loosely wrapped, in the coldest part of the refrigerator and used as soon as possible.

How to Cook Meat

Whatever type of meat is used and whatever method of cooking, the final result must be both moist and tender when served.

Expensive cuts of meat which are tender by nature are usually cooked by the dry-heat methods of roasting or shallow frying. The meat is seared by high heat on the outside to form a crust which contains the juices and natural tenderness of the meat. Slow cooking by moist heat – stewing or braising – is ideal for less tender cuts of meat as it softens any tough fibres and improves the flavour.

How to Tell When Meat is Cooked

Roast and Fried Meats The degree of cooking you prefer for roast or fried meats is very much a matter of individual taste. For small pieces of meat the French rely on touch, pressing steaks with their fingers: rare meat will be soft, medium will offer some resistance and well-done meat will feel firm to the touch. Larger joints can be tested with a meat thermometer or a skewer can be inserted into the joint and its temperature tested 30 seconds after it has been withdrawn. The table below gives a guide for testing roast meat.

Stage	Colour of meat when cut	Meat	Temperature on meat thermometer	Skewer
rare	deep pink	beef lamb liver kidneys	60 C/140 F	warm
medium	light pink	beef lamb veal	70 to 72 C/ 160 to 165 F	quite hot
well done	white	veal pork	75 to 77 C/ 170 to 175	very hot

Braised and Stewed Meat

The traditional French test for small pieces of stewed meat is that they are done when they can be cut with a spoon. For braised joints a skewer should be inserted and if it can be easily removed the joint is sufficiently tender.

How to Serve Meat

French ideas on serving depend both on the type of meat and how it is cooked. Roasts require expensive cuts, so they are usually reserved for festive occasions and given a variety of accompaniments, as in Roast Veal with Spring Vegetables. Choose a vegetable accompaniment to suit the type of meat – a delicate vegetable purée to accompany veal or robust red cabbage to complement the richness of pork.

Pot au Feu

Pot au Feu

The broth is served as soup followed by the meat and vegetables served with pickles, horseradish and mustard.

Pot au Feu stock (below) *or* a mixture of 3 litres/5 pints brown beef stock (page 18) *or* white veal stock (page 19) and 3 litres/5 pints water
1 (1.5-kg/3-lb) piece top rib of beef or chuck steak
1 (1.5-kg/3-lb) piece topside or silverside of beef
1.5 kg/2 lb beef marrow bones
450 g/1 lb onions, halved
450 g/1 lb carrots, halved and cut in 8-cm/3-in lengths
450 g/1 lb small turnips, quartered
450 g/1 lb leeks, cut in 8-cm/3-in lengths
6 stalks celery, cut in 8-cm/3-in lengths
salt and pepper to taste
50 g/2 oz vermicelli or very fine noodles *or* 1 small loaf French bread

POT AU FEU STOCK

1 kg/2 lb veal bones, cracked into 2 or 3 pieces
1 onion, quartered
1 large carrot, quartered
1 large bouquet garni
1 clove
salt to taste
10 peppercorns
6 litres/10 pints water

Prepare the Pot au Feu stock or combine the beef or veal stock and water and bring almost to the boil. Tie each cut of beef into a compact cylinder using trussing string and add the beef to the hot stock. Simmer for 2 to 3 hours until the meat is nearly tender. Wrap the marrow bones in muslin so the marrow does not fall out during cooking. Each type of vegetable may also be tied in muslin so it is easy to lift out after cooking. Add the marrow bones, onions and carrots to the stock and simmer for a further 20 minutes. Add the turnips, leeks, celery, salt and pepper and simmer for 30 minutes or until the meat is very tender.

If serving the broth with vermicelli or noodles, spoon 1 litre/2 pints broth into a large saucepan 10 minutes before the meat is cooked. Bring the broth to the boil, add the vermicelli or noodles and simmer for 5 minutes or until tender. If serving the broth with bread, cut the bread into 1-cm/½-in diagonal slices and toast in a moderate oven (180 C, 350 F, gas 4) for 10 to 15 minutes until golden brown. Remove the beef and vegetables from the broth and discard the trussing string. Carve the topside or silverside into fairly thick slices and arrange overlapping down the centre of a large platter. Cut the top rib or chuck steak in pieces and pile at each end. Arrange the vegetables around the meat. Cover the platter with foil and keep warm in a low oven (150 C, 300 F, gas 2).

Add the cooked vermicelli or noodles and their broth to the cooking liquid and skim off as much fat as possible. Reheat and taste for seasoning. If serving with toasted bread, unwrap the marrow bones and spread the bread with marrow. Place the bread in the soup bowls and pour the broth over it. If not using the marrow for bread, add the bones to the platter of meat and give guests spoons for scooping out the marrow. After serving the broth in soup bowls, serve the meat and vegetables. **Serves 10–12**

Pot au Feu Stock

If you don't have a heavy cleaver, ask a butcher to crack the bones. Place all the ingredients in a large saucepan. Bring slowly to the boil over a period of 20 to 30 minutes. Skim the stock often. Reduce the heat and simmer uncovered for 2½ to 3 hours, skimming occasionally. Strain before using in recipe above.

Beef Bourguignon

Boeuf à la Bourguignonne

One of the most popular of all French recipes, the best Beef Bourguignon needs good-quality stewing beef.

675 g/$1\frac{1}{2}$ lb chuck steak, cut in 3-cm/$1\frac{1}{4}$-in cubes
1 (225-g/8-oz) piece lean bacon, diced
4 tablespoons vegetable oil
16 pickling onions, peeled
225 g/8 oz mushrooms
3 tablespoons flour
300 ml/$\frac{1}{2}$ pint brown veal or beef stock (page 18)
salt and pepper to taste
croûtes (page 22)
1 tablespoon chopped parsley

Marinade

1 bottle red wine
1 onion, sliced
1 carrot, sliced
1 bouquet garni
1 clove garlic, crushed
6 peppercorns
2 cloves
10 juniper berries (optional)
pinch of salt
2 tablespoons vegetable oil

Mix all the ingredients for the marinade together in a non-metallic bowl and add the beef, pushing it under the liquid. Cover and chill for 24 to 48 hours, stirring occasionally. Put the bacon in a saucepan, cover generously with water and boil for 2 to 3 minutes. Drain and rinse with cold water. Drain the beef, reserving the marinade and the carrot and onion separately, and dry on absorbent kitchen paper.

Heat 2 tablespoons of the oil in a flameproof casserole and brown the beef a few pieces at a time. Add the bacon to the pan and fry until browned but not crisp. Remove from the pan, then sauté the onions and then the mushrooms until tender and lightly browned; remove. Discard excess fat from the casserole and add 6 tablespoons of the marinade. Bring to the boil, stirring to dissolve the pan juices, pour into a small bowl and reserve. In the same casserole, heat the remaining 2 tablespoons oil and fry the reserved onion and carrot from the marinade until soft but not browned. Stir in the flour and cook, stirring constantly, until the mixture is a rich brown. Do not burn. Stir in the remaining marinade, juices from the casserole, stock and a little salt and pepper.

Return the beef to the casserole and bring the stew to the boil. Cover tightly, reduce the heat and simmer for $2\frac{1}{2}$ to 3 hours until the meat is very tender. Alternatively cook the beef in a moderate oven (160 C. 325 F, gas 3). Lift the pieces of beef from the liquid and transfer to another casserole or large saucepan. Strain the sauce over them and add the bacon, onions and mushrooms. Simmer for 15 minutes or until the onions are tender and the flavours are blended. Taste and adjust the seasoning. Beef Bourguignon can be prepared to this point 2 days ahead, covered and refrigerated or frozen. It tastes best when prepared at least 1 day ahead. Reheat over medium heat or in a moderate oven (180 C, 350 F, gas 4). Serve the stew from the casserole or spoon into a shallow dish. Sprinkle with parsley and arrange croûtes around the edge. **Serves 4**

Pepper Steak

Steak au Poivre

For a stronger flavour, use more pepper. For a mild flavour, scrape the pepper of the steak before cooking.

2 tablespoons peppercorns
4 (2 to 2.5-cm/$\frac{3}{4}$ to 1-in thick) rump or fillet steaks
2 tablespoons vegetable oil
25 g/1 oz butter
salt to taste
3 tablespoons brandy
300 ml/$\frac{1}{2}$ pint single cream

Roughly crush the peppercorns in a pestle and mortar or with a rolling pin or the bottom of a heavy saucepan. Press them firmly into both sides of the steaks. Cover and chill for 2 to 3 hours. Heat the oil and butter in a large frying pan. Fry the steaks over high heat for 2 to 3 minutes on each side for rare. Sprinkle with salt after turning and remove from the frying pan. Discard the fat and return the steaks to the pan. Warm the brandy in a small pan and heat until hot but not boiling. Stand back, ignite the brandy and pour immediately over the steaks. Wait until the flames die down, then remove them and keep them warm. Add the cream to the pan and simmer for 2 to 3 minutes, stirring to dissolve the brown juices. Transfer the steaks to individual serving plates. Taste the sauce for seasoning, pour over the steaks and serve immediately. **Serves 4**

Beef Wellington

Place beef on duxelles and enclose with pastry.

Use egg glaze to attach decorative shapes.

Beef Wellington

Boeuf en Croûte

Work quickly when wrapping the beef so the butter in the brioche dough won't melt.

1 quantity brioche dough (page 121)
1 (1.5 to 1.75 kg/3 to 4-lb) fillet of beef
salt and pepper
2 tablespoons vegetable oil
duxelles (page 57)
1 egg beaten with a pinch of salt to glaze
1 bunch watercress to garnish

Prepare the brioche dough and let it rise. Chill until firm enough to roll out—at least 3 hours, or overnight.

Trim the fillet and tie into a compact shape with trussing string. Sprinkle with salt and pepper. Heat the oil in a large frying pan and brown the beef on all sides over high heat for 8 to 10 minutes. Cool completely. Meanwhile prepare the duxelles and chill.

Lightly grease a baking sheet. Roll out the brioche dough on a clean tea-towel to a rectangle 15 cm/6 in longer and wider than the trussed beef. Spread the dough with the cooled duxelles, leaving a 3-cm/2-in border. Remove the trussing string from the fillet and place upside down on the duxelles. Cut a 5-cm/2-in square from each corner of the dough and brush the edges of the rectangle with beaten egg. Lift one long edge of dough to the top of the fillet. Fold over the opposite edge to enclose fillet and press gently to seal. Fold up the ends to make a neat package. With the help of the tea-towel, roll the enclosed fillet over onto the prepared baking sheet so that the seam is underneath. Brush with beaten egg. Cut leaves and other decorative shapes from leftover dough and attach to the top of the pastry with beaten egg. Brush the decorations with beaten egg. Use a sharp knife to cut three equally spaced holes in the top of the dough. Insert a roll of foil or the smaller end of a plain icing nozzle in each hole to let steam escape. Cover and chill for 2 to 3 hours until the dough is firm. Beef Wellington can be prepared to this point 8 hours ahead, covered and refrigerated.

Preheat the oven to hot (220 C, 425 F, gas 7). Bake the Beef Wellington for 30 minutes or until the dough is browned and the beef cooked to rare (60 C/420 F on a meat thermometer). Check the pastry after 15 minutes and if it is becoming too brown, reduce the oven temperature to moderately hot (200 C, 400 F, gas 6). Transfer to a large platter and keep warm for 10 to 15 minutes to allow the juices to settle. Garnish with watercress and serve with Madeira sauce (page 72), handed separately. **Serves 6**

Beef Casserole with Olives and Vegetables

Boeuf en Daube

Tough cuts of meat cooked en daube should become tender enough to cut with a spoon.

1.5 kg/3 lb chuck steak or shin of beef
350 g/12 oz lean salt pork, cut in small pieces (optional)
1 pig's trotter, washed (optional)
675 g/1½ lb tomatoes, peeled, seeded and chopped *or* 1 (425-g/15-oz) can tomatoes, drained and chopped
450 g/1 lb carrots, sliced in thick rounds
pepper to taste
450 ml/12 fl oz white veal stock (page 19) *or* brown beef stock (page 18)
450 g/1 lb mushrooms, sliced
450 g/1 lb pickling onions, peeled
100 g/4 oz green olives, stoned
100 g/4 oz black olives, stoned

Marinade

2 tablespoons wine vinegar
450 ml/¾ pint red wine
1 onion, sliced
1 carrot, sliced
1 large bouquet garni
1 strip thinly pared orange peel
2 cloves garlic, crushed
6 peppercorns
1 clove
½ teaspoon coriander seeds
2 tablespoons olive oil

Mix together all the ingredients for the marinade in a deep non-metallic bowl. Add the beef, pushing it under the marinade, cover and refrigerate for 24 to 48 hours, stirring occasionally. In a large saucepan, generously cover the salt pork and pig's trotter, if using, with cold water. Boil for 10 minutes then drain, rinse with cold water and drain again. Preheat the oven to 150 C, 300 F, gas 2. Remove the beef from the marinade and tie the marinade vegetables, herbs, orange peel and spices in a piece of muslin. In a large flameproof casserole, layer the beef, pork and pig's trotter with tomatoes and carrots. Pour in the marinade. Add pepper, stock and the bag of vegetables. Do not add extra salt if you are using the salt pork as this will be salty enough. Gradually bring to the boil, cover tightly and cook in the oven for 2½ to 3 hours until the beef is very tender.

Remove the pig's trotter, pull the meat from the bone and shred with a fork. Return the meat to the casserole with the mushrooms, pickling onions and green and black olives. Cook for a further 15 to 20 minutes until the onions are done. Discard the muslin bag and taste the sauce for seasoning. Serve from the casserole or spoon into a bowl. This casserole can be made 2 days ahead, covered and refrigerated or frozen. Reheat in a moderate (180 C, 350 F, gas 4) oven or over medium heat on top of stove. Skim off the fat and taste for seasoning. **Serves 6–8**

Steak in Red Wine Sauce

Entrecôte Marchand de Vin

A respectable wine is a must for this sauce. Try a good Bordeaux and drink the rest with your steak.

1 tablespoon vegetable oil
15 g/½ oz butter
4 fillet *or* sirloin steaks, cut 2.5-cm/1-in thick
salt and pepper
3 shallots, finely chopped
1 clove garlic, finely chopped (optional)
300 ml/½ pint red wine
2 tablespoons chopped parsley
1 tablespoon chopped fresh herbs (chives, tarragon or basil)
1 bunch watercress

Heat the oil and butter in a large heavy frying pan. Fry the steaks over high heat for 2 to 3 minutes on each side for rare. Sprinkle with salt and pepper after turning. Transfer the steaks to a heatproof platter and keep warm in a cool (150 C, 300 F, gas 2) oven. Let the frying pan cool slightly, then add the shallots and garlic. Cook over medium heat for about 1 minute until the shallots begin to soften. Add the wine, stirring over medium heat to dissolve the brown juices on the bottom of the pan. Boil until the liquid is reduced by at least half and the flavour is concentrated. Remove from the heat and add the parsley and other herbs. Taste for seasoning. Pour the sauce over the steaks and serve garnished with watercress. **Serves 4**

Parsleyed Leg of Lamb

Gigot d'Agneau Persillé

Parsley coating gives a crisp brown crust to roast leg of lamb.

1 (1.75 to 2.25-kg/4 to 5-lb) leg of lamb
2 tablespoons vegetable oil
1 onion, quartered
1 carrot, quartered
salt and pepper
300 to 450 ml/$\frac{1}{2}$ to $\frac{3}{4}$ pint brown veal stock (page 18) *or* water
25 g/1 oz parsley, chopped
50 g/2 oz fresh white breadcrumbs
1 clove garlic, finely chopped
50 g/2 oz butter, melted
6 tablespoons white wine
1 bunch watercress

Preheat the oven to hot (230 C, 450 F, gas 8). Trim the skin and all but a thin layer of fat from the lamb. Pour the oil into a large roasting pan and add the onion and carrot. Place the lamb on top of these and sprinkle with salt and pepper. Roast for 10 to 15 minutes until browned. Reduce the oven temperature to moderately hot (200 C, 400 F, gas 6) and continue roasting. Allow 9 to 11 minutes per 450 g/1 lb for rare meat and 13 to 15 minutes per 450 g/1 lb for medium meat, including the first 10 to 15 minutes in the cooking time. Baste frequently, adding a little stock if the pan becomes too dry.

Mix the parsley, breadcrumbs and garlic together. Remove the lamb from the oven 10 minutes before the end of the cooking time and spread evenly with the breadcrumb mixture. Sprinkle with the melted butter, return to the oven for 10 more minutes or until the coating is lightly browned. Transfer the lamb to a platter and allow to stand in a warm place for 10 to 15 minutes before carving to let the juices settle.

To make the gravy, discard excess fat from the roasting pan, reserving the onion and carrot and add the wine and 1 cup of stock. Bring to the boil, stirring to dissolve any brown juices, and simmer for 5 to 10 minutes to concentrate the flavour. Strain into a small saucepan, skimming off excess fat. Bring to the boil and taste for seasoning. Cover and keep warm over very low heat until ready to serve. Place the lamb on a platter and garnish with watercress. Serve the gravy separately. **Serves 6**

Lamb Chop and Potato Casserole

Côtes de Mouton Champvallon

A simple dish that needs no last-minute attention.

4 lamb chops
1 tablespoon vegetable oil
40 g/1$\frac{1}{2}$ oz butter
2 large onions, thinly sliced
6 medium-sized potatoes, thinly sliced
salt and pepper to taste
pinch of chopped fresh thyme or dried thyme
4 tablespoons chopped parsley
1 clove garlic, halved
450 ml/$\frac{3}{4}$ pint white veal stock (page 19)

Preheat the oven to moderate (180 C, 350 F, gas 4). Trim excess fat and gristle from the chops. Heat the oil and 25 g/1 oz of the butter in a large frying pan and brown the chops on both sides over medium heat. Remove the chops and discard all but 2 tablespoons of the fat. Sauté the onions until just transparent, then remove and mix with the potatoes, salt, pepper, thyme and 2 tablespoons of the parsley.

Generously grease a 2-litre/3$\frac{1}{2}$-pint shallow baking dish and rub with garlic. Spoon half the potato mixture into the dish and place the chops on top. Cover with the remaining potato mixture. Pour in enough stock to just cover the potatoes. Dot with the remaining butter. Bake uncovered for 45 to 60 minutes until the potatoes and chops are tender when pierced with a fork. The top of the potatoes should be golden brown and most of the liquid should have been absorbed. Sprinkle with the remaining parsley and serve from the baking dish. **Serves 4**

Lamb and Vegetable Stew

Navarin Printanier

This dish is best made in springtime, with as many fresh vegetables as possible.

675 g/1½ lb boned shoulder of lamb, cubed
salt and pepper
2 tablespoons vegetable oil
12 pickling onions, peeled
2 tablespoons flour
1 tablespoon concentrated tomato purée
1 clove garlic, finely chopped
1 bouquet garni
750 ml to 1 litre/1¼ to 1¾ pints white veal stock (page 19), brown beef stock (page 18) or chicken stock (page 19)
2 tomatoes, peeled, seeded and chopped
1 new carrot, peeled, *or* 2 large carrots, quartered
1 turnip, cut in eighths
675 g/1½ lb small new potatoes *or* 3 to 4 large potatoes, quartered
100 g/4 oz fresh peas, blanched, *or* 1 (100-g/4-oz) packet frozen peas
2 tablespoons chopped parsley

Sprinkle the lamb with salt and pepper. Heat the oil in a large flameproof casserole. Brown the lamb over medium heat a few pieces at a time, on all sides. Add the onions to the pan and sauté until browned. Remove and stir in the flour. Stir over medium heat until foaming. Add the tomato purée, garlic, bouquet garni and 750 ml/1¼ pints stock. Return the lamb to the casserole, adding more stock to cover the lamb if necessary. Bring to the boil, cover tightly, reduce the heat and simmer for 1 hour. Skim off any fat. Add the tomatoes and carrots with more stock to cover, if needed. Cover and simmer for a further 30 minutes. Add the turnip, potatoes and browned onions and simmer for 10 minutes longer. Add the fresh peas and simmer for a final 20 minutes or until the meat is tender. Frozen peas should be added after turnips and potatoes have simmered for 20 minutes and should be cooked for 8 to 10 minutes.

Discard the bouquet garni and taste for seasoning. The sauce should have some body but will not be thick enough to coat a spoon. If necessary, remove the meat and vegetables and boil the sauce to thicken slightly. Return the meat and vegetables to the sauce. Sprinkle with parsley and serve from the casserole. **Serves 4**

Veal Chops Dijonnaise

Côtes de Veau à la Dijonnaise

(Illustrated on front endpaper)

1 tablespoon vegetable oil
1 (100-g/4-oz) piece lean bacon, cut in 5-mm/¼-in cubes
16 pickling onions, peeled
4 large veal chops
salt and pepper to taste
1 tablespoon flour
6 tablespoons white wine
6 tablespoons white veal stock or chicken stock (both page 18)
1 bouquet garni
3 tablespoons single cream
2 tablespoons French mustard
1 tablespoon chopped parsley

Preheat the oven to moderate (180 C, 350 F, gas 4). Heat the oil in a large frying pan and fry the bacon until browned. Remove from the pan and sauté the onions until browned. Remove from the pan. Sprinkle the veal chops with salt and pepper and brown on both sides over medium-high heat. Remove the chops and discard all but 2 tablespoons of the fat. Stir in the flour and cook, stirring constantly until foaming. Stir in the wine, stock, bouquet garni and pepper to taste. Do not add salt at this stage as the bacon may be salty enough to season the dish. Bring just to the boil, stirring occasionally. Return the chops and bacon to the frying pan, cover and bake in the oven for 25 to 30 minutes. Alternatively simmer gently on top of the stove. Add the onions and cook for a further 15 minutes or until the chops and onions are tender.

Overlap the chops on a platter, cover with foil and keep warm. Taste the sauce and, if necessary, reduce until it coats the back of a spoon and the flavour is concentrated. Add the cream, heat until nearly boiling then remove from heat and stir in the mustard. Do not boil the mustard or it will become bitter. Discard the bouquet garni. Adjust the seasoning and spoon with the onion and bacon garnish over the chops. Sprinkle with parsley before serving. **Serves 4**

Lamb and Vegetable Stew (above).

Roast Veal with Spring Vegetables

Rôti de Veau Printanier

The same spring vegetables are also good with roast pork or lamb.

1 (1.5- to 1.75-kg/3- to 4-lb) rolled veal roast
50 g/2 oz butter, softened
2 teaspoons fresh chopped mixed herbs such as thyme, oregano and rosemary
salt and pepper
450 to 600 ml/¾ to 1 pint white veal stock (page 19)
250 ml/8 fl oz white wine
SPRING VEGETABLES
1 lb new carrots
2 teaspoons sugar
salt and pepper
75 g/3 oz tablespoons butter
450 g/1 lb French beans, cut in 8-cm/3-in lengths
24 pickling onions, peeled
675 g/1½ lb small new potatoes
2 tablespoons chopped parsley

Preheat the oven to moderate (180 C, 350 F, gas 4). Trim the veal and tie into a compact cylinder with trussing string. Spread with butter and sprinkle with the herbs, salt and pepper. Place in a roasting tin with 6 tablespoons stock and half the white wine. For slightly pink meat (70 C/160 F, on a meat thermometer), roast for 30 minutes per pound, basting frequently and adding more stock if the pan gets too dry. Prepare the vegetables (see below) and set aside until the meat is done. Let the roast rest on a platter in a warm place for 15 minutes to allow the juices to settle.

To make the gravy, add the remaining stock and wine to the roasting tin and bring to the boil, stirring. Strain into a small saucepan. Bring to the boil and taste again, if necessary, continuing to boil until the flavour is concentrated. Taste and adjust the seasoning. Discard the trussing strings and carve the veal into slices. Overlap the slices down the centre of a large platter and arrange the vegetables round the veal. Spoon a little gravy over the meat and serve the remaining gravy separately.

Spring Vegetables

Peel the carrots and put in a medium saucepan with water to cover, 1 teaspoon of the sugar, a pinch of salt and 15 g/½ oz butter. Boil uncovered for 15 to 20 minutes until nearly all the liquid has evaporated and the carrots are tender. Cook the beans in boiling salted water for 10 to 12 minutes until just tender. Drain, rinse with cold water and drain thoroughly. Melt 25 g/1 oz butter in a heavy frying pan. Add the onions, the remaining 1 teaspoon sugar and a pinch of salt and pepper. Cook over low heat for 15 to 20 minutes, shaking the pan occasionally, until the onions are tender and lightly browned. Cook the potatoes in boiling salted water for 15 to 20 minutes until just tender then drain.

Just before serving, reheat each vegetable separately over low heat, adding 1 tablespoon butter and a pinch of salt and pepper to both the beans and the potatoes. When reheating the vegetables in butter, shake the pan instead of stirring to prevent the vegetables from breaking up. Add 1 tablespoon of chopped parsley to both the carrots and to the potatoes. **Serves 6–8**

Roast Veal Orloff

Rôti de Veau Orloff

Named after Prince Alexis Fedorovich Orlov, Russian ambassador to France in the 19th century.

1 (1.5- to 2-kg/3½- to 4-lb) boneless veal roast
40 g/1½ oz butter
salt and pepper to taste
250 ml/8 fl oz white wine
350 ml/12 fl oz white veal stock (page 19)
thick basic white sauce (page 69) made with 4 cups milk
1 quantity duxelles (below)
2 egg yolks
½ teaspoon French mustard
50 g/2 oz grated Gruyère cheese *or* 25 g/1 oz grated Parmesan cheese
150 ml/¼ pint milk or single cream
ONION PURÉE
5 medium onions, thinly sliced
40 g/1½ oz butter
salt and pepper to taste

Preheat the oven to moderate (180 C, 350 F, gas 4). Trim the veal and tie into a compact cylinder with trussing string. Spread with butter and sprinkle with salt and pepper. Place in a roasting tin and pour in 6 tablespoons each wine and stock. For slightly pink meat (70 C, 160 F, on meat thermometer), roast for 30 minutes per pound, basting frequently and adding more stock if the pan gets dry.

Prepare the onion purée. In a large heavy saucepan, generously cover the onions with cold water. Boil for 5 minutes, then drain. Melt the butter in the same pan and add the onions, salt and pepper. Cover with buttered foil and the pan lid. Cook over low heat for 10 to 15 minutes until the onions are very soft, but do not allow to brown. Press the mixture through a sieve or purée in a food processor or liquidiser. Return to the saucepan and cook for a few minutes stirring constantly, until nearly all the moisture has evaporated. Remove the meat from the pan and leave to stand in a warm place. Stir 2 tablespoons of the basic white sauce into the duxelles and taste for seasoning. Stir 6 tablespoons basic white sauce into the onion purée; taste for seasoning.

Discard the trussing strings and carve the meat in fairly thick slices. Spread alternate slices with the onion purée and duxelles mixtures and place together to reform the shape of the roast. Spread any leftover duxelles and onion purée mixtures on top of the meat. Bring the remaining white sauce to the boil, remove from the heat and beat in the egg yolks. Stir in the mustard and half the cheese. If necessary add a little milk, but the sauce should be quite thick. Taste for seasoning. Cover the top of the meat with a third of the sauce. Thin the remaining sauce with enough milk or single cream so it is just thick enough to coat the back of a spoon. Taste for seasoning. Spoon the sauce over the meat to coat both the meat and the platter. Sprinkle with the remaining cheese. Place the platter under a preheated grill until the sauce is bubbling and browned. **Serves 6–8**

Duxelles

Duxelles

25 g/1 oz butter
2 shallots, finely chopped
450 g/1 lb mushrooms, finely chopped
1 tablespoon chopped parsley
salt and pepper

Melt the butter in a frying pan. Add the shallots and stir over medium heat until soft but not browned. Add the mushrooms and cook over high heat, stirring often, until all the liquid is evaporated. Remove from the heat and add the parsley. Season to taste with salt and pepper.

Veal Stew with Cream

Blanquette de Veau

450 g/1 lb boneless shoulder of veal, cut in 5-cm/2-in pieces
1 kg/2 lb breast of veal including bones, cut in chunks
2 onions, quartered
1 clove
2 carrots, quartered
1 bouquet garni
green top of 1 leek (optional)
1.75 litres/3 pints white veal stock (page 19) or water
salt and pepper
225 g/8 oz mushrooms, stalks removed and quartered if large
juice of $\frac{1}{2}$ lemon
65 g/$2\frac{1}{2}$ oz butter
24 pickling onions, peeled
2 tablespoons flour
150 ml/$\frac{1}{4}$ pint single cream
pinch of nutmeg

In a large saucepan, generously cover the veal shoulder and breast with cold water. Bring to the boil, reduce the heat and simmer for 5 minutes, skimming frequently. Drain and rinse the veal with warm water. Place in a large flameproof casserole with the quartered onions, clove, carrots, bouquet garni, leek and enough stock or water to just cover. Season with salt and pepper, cover and bring to the boil. Simmer, skimming occasionally, for $1\frac{1}{4}$ to $1\frac{1}{2}$ hours until the veal is very tender.

In a medium saucepan, combine 5 mm/$\frac{1}{4}$ in water, the mushrooms, salt, pepper and 1 teaspoon lemon juice. Cover and cook over high heat for 5 minutes or until the mushrooms are tender. Set aside and add the cooking liquid to the simmering blanquette. Melt 25 g/1 oz of the butter in a large shallow saucepan. Add the pickling onions with salt and pepper. Cover and cook over very low heat for 15 to 20 minutes, shaking the pan occasionally to turn the onions until they are tender.

When the veal is tender, remove from the pan, reserving the broth. Melt the remaining butter in a medium saucepan and stir in the flour. Cook, stirring constantly, until foaming but not browned. Remove from the heat and strain in the reserved broth. Bring to the boil, stirring constantly, reduce the heat and simmer for 10 to 15 minutes until the sauce is thick enough to coat the back of a spoon. Stir in the cream, then add the meat, onions and mushrooms to the sauce. Season to taste with a little more lemon juice, nutmeg, salt and pepper. Warm over low heat for 5 to 10 minutes to blend the flavours. Serve in a shallow serving dish with plain rice or Rice Pilaf (page 85). **Serves 6**

Stuffed Pork Tenderloin Chasseur

Filet Mignon de Porc Farci Chasseur

3 pork fillets, total weight 675 g to 1 kg/1½ to 2 lb
25 g/1 oz butter
2 tablespoons flour
150 ml/¼ pint white wine
600 ml/1 pint white or brown veal stock (page 19 or 18)
3 teaspoons concentrated tomato purée
2 shallots, finely chopped
salt and pepper
225 g/8 oz mushrooms, thinly sliced
STUFFING
25 g/1 oz butter
1 onion, finely chopped
225 g/8 oz pork sausagemeat
1 tablespoon chopped parsley
1 teaspoon mixed fresh herbs such as sage, thyme and marjoram or ½ teaspoon mixed dried herbs
50 g/2 oz fresh white breadcrumbs
salt and pepper
1 egg, lightly beaten

First prepare the stuffing. Melt the butter in a saucepan and cook the onion over medium heat until soft but not browned. Remove from the heat and stir in the sausagemeat, parsley, mixed herbs, breadcrumbs and plenty of salt and pepper. Stir in the egg to bind. The mixture should be highly seasoned.

Using a sharp knife, split the tenderloins lengthways two-thirds of the way through. Open them flat and place between 2 sheets of greaseproof paper and pound each with a mallet or rolling pin to flatten. Sandwich the three tenderloins with two layers of stuffing and tie the meat into a neat loaf shape with trussing string. Heat the butter in a flameproof casserole. Add the pork and brown on all sides. Remove the pork, stir in the flour and cook until lightly browned. Add the wine, stock, tomato purée, shallots, salt and pepper. Return the pork to the casserole, cover and bring just to the boil. Cook in a moderate oven (180 C, 350 F, gas 4) for 1½ to 2 hours until very tender. Add the mushrooms 10 minutes before the end of the cooking time. Transfer the pork to a carving board, cover and keep warm.

Strain the cooking liquid into a saucepan and boil until thick enough to coat the back of a spoon. Discard the trussing string from the meat and carve into slices. Arrange the slices overlapping on a platter. Spoon the mushrooms over the meat, top with a little sauce and serve the rest of the sauce separately. **Serves 6**

Loin of Pork with Caramelised Apples

Carré de Porc Normand

Apples, Calvados and cream are the traditional ingredients of Normandy cooking.

1 tablespoon vegetable oil
15 g/½ oz butter
1 (1-kg/2-lb) loin of pork, rolled and tied
2 medium onions, sliced
2 cooking apples, peeled, cored and sliced
3 tablespoons Calvados or other brandy
1 tablespoon flour
600 ml/1 pint white veal stock or chicken stock (both page 19)
salt and pepper
25 g/1 oz butter
2 green-skinned eating apples, unpeeled, cut in slices
2 tablespoons sugar
4 tablespoons single or double cream

Preheat the oven to moderate (180 C, 350 F, gas 4). Heat the oil and butter in a large flameproof casserole. Brown the pork on all sides over medium heat. Remove from the pan. Add the onions and cook until soft but not browned, stirring occasionally. Add the cooking apple slices and continue cooking over medium heat until the apples and onions are golden brown. Return the pork to the casserole and flame with the Calvados or brandy. Stir the flour into the cooking liquid and add the stock, salt and pepper and bring to the boil; cover and cook in the oven for 1½ to 2 hours until the meat is tender.

Meanwhile prepare the caramelised apple slices. Heat the butter in a frying pan. Dip one side of each apple slice in sugar and cook sugar side down in hot butter over high heat for 4 to 5 minutes until the sugar is caramelised. Sprinkle the remaining sugar over the apples. Turn over and cook for a further 4 to 5 minutes. Do not overcook or the apples will be mushy. Remove the pork from the casserole, cover with foil and keep warm. Strain the sauce into a medium saucepan, pressing to purée the apples and onion. Boil until thick enough to coat a spoon. Add the cream, bring almost to the boil and taste for seasoning. Carve the pork in slices and arrange on a platter. Spoon the sauce over the pork and garnish with caramelised apple slices. **Serves 4**

Loin of Pork with Caramelised Apples and braised red cabbage (above).

Cassoulet

Cassoulet

A traditional hearty meat and bean stew which originated in the Languedoc region of southern France.

1 kg/2 lb haricot beans
1 carrot, quartered
1 onion, halved
4 cloves
2 bouquets garni
salt and pepper
1 (175-g/8-oz) piece lean salt pork, rind scored deeply
1 small (1.5- to 1.75-kg/3½- to 4-lb) duck, cut in 6 pieces
2 tablespoons melted lard or vegetable oil
450 g/1 lb shoulder or breast of lamb, cubed
450 g/1 lb boneless pork loin or shoulder, cubed
2 onions, chopped
4 cloves garlic, chopped
75 ml/2½ fl oz white wine
4 medium tomatoes, peeled, seeded, chopped (page 10) *or* 1 (396-g/14-oz) can tomatoes, drained and chopped
350 g/12 oz Toulouse or fresh garlic sausage

Place the beans, carrot, onion studded with the cloves, and one of the bouquet garni in a large saucepan. Add water to cover and simmer for 1 to 1¼ hours until the beans are almost tender, seasoning with salt and pepper halfway through the cooking time. Drain the beans, discarding the onion, carrot and bouquet garni and reserve the cooking liquid to add to the meat.

Generously cover the salt pork with cold water in a large saucepan. Boil for 10 minutes, then drain and rinse with cold water. Sprinkle the duck with salt and pepper. Heat the lard or oil in a large frying pan or flameproof casserole and brown the duck pieces on all sides over medium heat. Lower the heat and cook for 10 to 15 minutes longer until all the fat is rendered. Remove the duck and pour off all but 2 tablespoons of fat. Sprinkle the lamb pieces with salt and pepper and brown a few at a time in the fat. Sprinkle the pork cubes with salt and pepper and brown these in the remaining fat. Stir in the onions and sauté until lightly browned. Add the garlic for the last few seconds. Add the wine, stirring to dissolve any brown juices.

In a very large deep casserole, layer the beans, duck, lamb, pork and tomatoes, ending with beans. Add the remaining bouquet garni and place the salt pork on top. Add the onion mixture and just enough reserved bean liquid to cover the beans. Do not add salt as the salt pork is quite salty. Cover and bake in a cool oven (150 C, 300 F, gas 2) for 2½ to 3 hours until the meat is nearly tender. If the mixture becomes dry during cooking, add more liquid. If it is too soupy, remove the lid. Add the sausage and cook for 1 further hour. Remove the salt pork and sausage, slice and return to the casserole. Taste for seasoning. Increase the oven temperature to moderately hot (190 C, 375 F, gas 5) and bake for 45 minutes longer to brown. Discard the bouquet garni and serve from the casserole.
Serves 8–10

Calf's Liver with Onions

Foie de Veau à la Lyonnaise

'Lyonnaise' refers to a garnish of onions cooked in butter.

100 g/4 oz butter
8 onions, thinly sliced
salt and pepper
2 tablespoons vegetable oil
675 g/1½ lb calves' or lambs' liver

Melt 25 g/1 oz of the butter in a large heavy shallow saucepan. Add the onions and season with salt and pepper. Cover with a piece of buttered foil, then the pan lid. Cook over low heat, stirring occasionally, for 20 to 30 minutes until the onions are very soft. Remove the lid and foil and continue cooking onions until light golden. Do not allow to burn. Taste and season.

Heat the oil and 25 g/1 oz butter in a large frying pan. Sauté the liver for 2 to 3 minutes on each side until lightly browned for medium rare meat or cook a few minutes longer for medium to well-cooked meat. Arrange the liver on a serving plate. Reheat the onions and spoon them over the liver. Heat the remaining butter in a small pan and cook until nut brown. Pour the browned butter over the onions and serve at once.
Serves 4–6

Sautéed Sweetbreads

Ris de Veau Panés

This luxurious garnish is a perfect match for delicate sweetbreads.

675 g/$1\frac{1}{2}$ lb lamb's sweetbreads
1 slice lemon
salt
50 g/2 oz flour
$\frac{1}{2}$ teaspoon salt
$\frac{1}{4}$ teaspoon pepper
75 to 100 g/3 to 4 oz butter
1 (5-mm/$\frac{1}{4}$-in) slice prosciutto or uncooked smoked ham, finely diced (about 100 g/4 oz)
2 medium potatoes, boiled and cubed
100 g/4 oz mushrooms, thinly sliced
2 tomatoes, peeled, seeded and chopped
1 tablespoon chopped parsley

Soak the sweetbreads for 2 to 3 hours in a bowl of cold water, changing the water once or twice. Drain, rinse with cold water and drain again. Place the sweetbreads in a large saucepan and cover with plenty of cold water. Add the lemon and a pinch of salt. Bring slowly to the boil, skimming occasionally, then reduce the heat and simmer for 5 minutes. Drain the sweetbreads and rinse with cold water. Peel, removing ducts, and press between 2 plates with a 1-kg/2-lb weight on top. Chill for 1 hour.

Mix the flour with the salt and pepper. Cut the sweetbreads into diagonal 1-cm/$\frac{1}{2}$-in slices. Lightly coat the pieces of sweetbread with the flour mixture. Heat 50 g/2 oz of the butter in a frying pan. Fry the sweetbreads over medium heat for 8 to 10 minutes until tender and golden brown on both sides. Remove from the pan. Add the ham and potatoes and cook over medium heat, stirring occasionally, until golden brown, adding more butter, if necessary. Remove the ham and potatoes, cover with foil and keep warm. Add 25 g/1 oz more butter to the pan and cook the mushrooms and tomatoes over high heat, stirring constantly for 5 minutes or until the mushrooms are tender and the tomatoes pulpy. Taste for seasoning. Return the sweetbreads to the pan, turning to coat with the sauce. Reduce the heat and cook for a further 2 to 3 minutes to blend the flavours. Gently stir in the potatoes and ham. Transfer to a serving dish and sprinkle with parsley. **Serves 4**

Sautéed Kidneys with Mustard

Rognons Sautés à la Moutarde

This recipe can be cooked in a chafing dish at the table.

3 to 4 veal kidneys or 6 to 8 lambs' kidneys (total weight 675 g/$1\frac{1}{2}$ lb)
2 tablespoons vegetable oil
25 g/1 oz butter
3 tablespoons brandy
150 ml/$\frac{1}{4}$ pint single or double cream
salt and pepper
2 to 3 teaspoons French mustard
1 tablespoon chopped parsley

Skin the kidneys, if necessary, and cut out the core with scissors or a sharp knife. Cut the veal kidneys into 1-cm/$\frac{1}{2}$-in slices or the lamb's kidneys in half to form crescents. In a chafing dish or medium-sized frying pan heat the oil and butter until very hot. Add half the kidneys; if using lamb kidneys, place them cut side down. Sauté for 1 to 2 minutes until browned on the outside but still rare in the centre. Remove from the pan. Add more butter and oil, if needed, and quickly sauté the remaining kidneys. Remove the kidneys and drain in a colander placed over a plate. Return the kidneys to the pan and heat quickly until very hot. Flame with brandy, stir in the cream and season with salt and pepper. Bring just to the boil, remove from the heat and stir in the mustard. Warm over a low heat for 1 to 2 minutes to blend the flavours. Do not boil the mustard or it will become bitter. Sprinkle with parsley and serve immediately. **Serves 4**

Eggs

Eggs are the most versatile of all ingredients. They can be boiled, poached, fried, scrambled or cooked as an omelette. Their mild flavour makes them the perfect partner for other flavours ranging from ham to chicken, fish, shellfish and cooked vegetables.

How to Cook Eggs

No matter how you cook them, there are two basic facts about eggs: they cook quickly at a relatively low temperature (about 60 C/140 F) and fierce heat toughens them. Use low heat in cooking, except for omelettes which are only partly cooked, and for soufflés where the eggs are protected by the dish. Respect cooking times or the result will be tough, overcooked whites and dry yolks. Thirty seconds can make the difference between a perfect egg and one that is overdone. For the same reason, hot egg dishes should be served as soon as they are ready because they will continue to cook in the residual heat of the the dish.

Judging the point at which an egg is perfectly cooked takes a little experience and a precise time cannot be given except for hard-boiled eggs. French cooks tell by appearance and sometimes by touch, especially for poached eggs. To French taste, eggs should be soft. Folded omelettes should be slightly runny in the centre, whilst scrambled eggs should be soft and moist. For poached eggs the white should be set and the yolk runny.

How to Serve Eggs

The French do not serve eggs for breakfast, but prefer them as the first course of a meal. They can also be the main course of a light lunch or supper, usually in the form of an omelette. The number of eggs to serve per person depends on the cooking method and on their role in the menu. A single poached, baked or hard-boiled egg is enough for a first course, especially if accompanied by a substantial garnish, but two are needed for a main course. For omelettes or scrambled eggs, two eggs per person are a minimum even as a starter.

For a dinner party, eggs need special treatment. Poached or hard-boiled eggs need a sauce to cover their pale appearance. Serve scrambled or poached eggs on toast or fried bread, or in tartlet shells to give a crisp contrast to the soft egg. The most dramatic, if risky, presentation is a soufflé, but one well worth the effort.

Cheese Soufflé (page 66).

How to Poach Eggs

Eggs for poaching must be very fresh or the white will detach from the yolk in strings. Fill a wide, shallow non-aluminium saucepan two-thirds full of water. Add about three tablespoons vinegar for each litre (about 2 pints). Bring the water to a rolling boil. Break an egg into a bubbling portion of the water – the bubbles spin the egg so the white sets around the yolk. Repeat with up to five eggs. Reduce the heat and poach for 3 to 4 minutes. Remove the eggs with a slotted spoon. The whites should just be firm and the yolks still soft. Place the poached eggs in a bowl of cold water. When they are cool, remove and trim any ragged edges with a knife or scissors. Return the eggs to the water. Reheat by standing the eggs in warm water for a few minutes.

How to Hard Boil Eggs

To help prevent cracking use eggs which are at room temperature. Put enough water to cover the eggs generously in a large non-aluminium saucepan. Bring to the boil and carefully lower the eggs into the boiling water with a spoon. Return to the boil, lower the heat and simmer for 10 to 12 minutes, counting the cooking time from when the water returns to the boil. Be careful not to simmer the eggs for more than 12 minutes as overcooked eggs will have a black line around the yolk. Drain the eggs. Cover with cold water and leave until cool. To peel, gently tap the eggs all over to crack the shell, then remove the shell with the skin. Peeled eggs can be kept at room temperature in a bowl of cold water for up to 24 hours but are best left unpeeled until needed. Chilled hard-boiled eggs become tough.

Scrambled Eggs with Fresh Herbs

Oeufs Brouillés aux Fines Herbes

Fresh herbs make all the difference to this simple dish.

4 slices bread
2 tablespoons vegetable oil
100 g/4 oz butter
8 eggs
salt and pepper to taste
2 tablespoons chopped mixed fresh herbs (parsley, chervil, chives or tarragon)

Cut 4 rounds from the bread with a 7.5-cm/3-in biscuit cutter. Heat the oil and 15 g/1 oz of the butter in a frying pan and fry the bread rounds until golden brown on both sides. Drain on absorbent kitchen paper, arrange on a serving dish and keep warm.

Whisk the eggs with salt and pepper until slightly frothy, then quickly beat in the herbs. Heat the remaining butter in a medium-sized heavy pan. Add the eggs and stir constantly with a wooden spoon over a low heat for at least 3 minutes until they begin to thicken. The slower the eggs cook, the smooother they will be. Cook to desired consistency, remembering that the eggs will continue cooking in the pan after it has been removed from heat. Spoon the eggs on to fried bread rounds and serve immediately. **Serves 4**

Pipérade

Pipérade

This traditional Basque recipe is a more elaborate version of scrambled eggs.

3 tablespoons olive oil
1 onion, thinly sliced
2 tomatoes, peeled, seeded and chopped
1 clove garlic, crushed
salt and pepper
1 red or green pepper, cored, seeded and cut into 5-mm/¼-in dice
6 eggs, lightly beaten

Heat the oil in a medium-sized pan. Add the onion and sauté until soft but not browned. Add the tomatoes, garlic, salt and pepper to taste and cook over low heat for 15 minutes or until thick and pulpy, stirring occasionally. Stir in the pepper and cook for a further 5 minutes or until the pepper is soft. Taste and adjust the seasoning.

Beat the eggs with a fork until frothy and stir into the warm tomato mixture. Stir constantly over low heat until the eggs have thickened but are still soft. This should take at least 5 minutes, or the eggs may be watery instead of smooth. Remember that the mixture will continue cooking in the pan after it is removed from heat. Serve immediately. **Serves 2**

Eggs Benedict

Oeufs Bénédict

Like all dishes with Hollandaise Sauce, Eggs Bénédict should be served warm rather than hot.

6 poached eggs (page 63)
250 ml/8 fl oz Hollandaise Sauce (page 75)
6 thick slices ham
2 tablespoons sherry or Madeira
1 truffle, drained if canned, *or* 3 black olives
3 muffins or 6 slices bread
15 g/½ oz butter

Keep cooked eggs warm in a bowl of warm water. Keep the Hollandaise Sauce warm in a water bath (page 75). Set the oven at cool (120 C, 250 F, gas 1). Cut rounds from the ham the same size as the muffins or, if using bread, cut into 7.5-cm/3-in rounds. Place the ham on an ovenproof plate and pour over the sherry or Madeira. Tightly cover with foil and place in the oven to warm.

Cut the truffle into 6 slices or halve the olives, discarding the stones. Split and toast the muffins or toast the bread and cut into 7.5-cm/3-in rounds. Spread the muffins or toast with butter and place a slice of ham on top. Drain the eggs and dry thoroughly on absorbent kitchen paper. Place on the ham and arrange on a warm serving plate. Spoon the Hollandaise Sauce over the eggs and top with a slice of truffle or olive half. Serve immediately. **Serves 6 as a starter or 3 as a main course**

Poached Eggs Florentine

Oeufs Pochés Florentine

Florentine refers to the spinach, supposedly introduced to France from Florence by the princess Catherine de Medici.

8 very lightly poached eggs (page 63)
1.25 kg/2½ lb fresh spinach *or* 575 g/1¼ lb frozen leaf spinach
25 g/1 oz butter
salt and pepper
pinch of nutmeg
thin basic white sauce (page 69) made with 475 ml/16 fl oz milk
2 egg yolks
75 g/3 oz grated Gruyère cheese *or* 25 g/1 oz grated Parmesan cheese
1 teaspoon French mustard
4 tablespoons milk (optional)

Place the cooked eggs in a bowl of cold water. If using fresh spinach, remove the stems and wash the leaves thoroughly. Fill a large saucepan three-quarters full of lightly salted water. Bring to the boil then plunge in the spinach. Bring back to the boil and continue to boil for about 5 minutes or until the leaves are wilted, stirring occasionally. If using frozen spinach, cook according to the instructions on the packet. Drain the spinach, rinse with cold water and squeeze to extract as much water as possible.

Just before serving, transfer the eggs to a bowl of warm water to heat them. Grease a shallow 1.4-litre/2½-pint ovenproof dish and preheat the grill. Melt the butter in a saucepan, add the spinach and toss with a fork until thoroughly heated. Season to taste with salt, pepper and nutmeg and spread the spinach in the prepared dish. Drain the eggs on absorbent kitchen paper. Arrange the eggs on top of the spinach and cover to keep warm.

Bring the white sauce to the boil, remove from the heat and beat in the egg yolks, two-thirds of the cheese, mustard, and salt and pepper to taste. The sauce should thickly coat the spoon; if too thick, stir in up to 4 tablespoons more milk. Spoon the sauce over the eggs and spinach, sprinkle with the remaining cheese and brown quickly under the grill. Poached Eggs Florentine can be kept hot for 10 to 15 minutes in a water bath (page 16) but the eggs easily overcook. **Serves 8 as a starter or 4 as a main course**

Cheese Soufflé

Soufflé au Fromage

(Illustrated on page 62)
A mixture of Parmesan and Gruyère is perfect for this soufflé. You can also use mature Cheddar.

2 tablespoons dried breadcrumbs (optional)
40 g/1½ oz butter
15 g/½ oz flour
250 ml/8 fl oz milk
salt and pepper
4 egg yolks
65 g/2½ oz grated cheese
1 teaspoon prepared mustard *or* ¼ teaspoon dry mustard
6 egg whites

Preheat the oven to hot (220 C, 425 F, gas 7). Generously butter a 1.4-litre/2½-pint soufflé dish and sprinkle with the breadcrumbs, if using. Melt the butter in a medium-sized saucepan and whisk in the flour. Cook until the mixture foams; do not allow to brown. Whisk in the milk and bring to a boil, stirring constantly. Season to taste, then reduce the heat and simmer for 2 minutes. Remove from the heat and beat the egg yolks into the hot sauce until thickened. Cool slightly, then beat in 50 g/2 oz of the cheese with the mustard. Taste and adjust the seasoning. The mixture should be highly seasoned as the egg whites will be added later.

Cheese Soufflé can be prepared to this point 3 or 4 hours ahead. Rub the surface of the cheese mixture with butter to prevent a skin forming. If made ahead, cover and refrigerate.

Thirty minutes before serving, preheat the oven. Whip the egg whites until stiff. If made ahead, heat the cheese mixture over a low heat, whisking constantly, until hot to the touch. Do not heat too long or the cheese will become stringy. Thoroughly mix a quarter of the stiff egg whites into the hot cheese mixture then lightly fold the cheese mixture into the remaining egg whites. Pour into the prepared dish and sprinkle with the remaining cheese. Bake for 12 to 15 minutes until the soufflé is risen and brown. Serve immediately. **Serves 4**

Country-style Omelette

Omelette Paysanne

This hearty omelette can be made several hours ahead and served cold.

100 g/4 oz back bacon, diced
1 medium potato, diced
1 small onion, diced
2 tablespoons finely chopped parsley
4 eggs
salt and pepper
25 g/1 oz butter

Fry the bacon in a medium-sized frying pan until the fat begins to run. Stir in the potato and onion and cook over medium heat, stirring constantly until browned and tender. Add the parsley, remove from the heat and keep warm. Use a fork to beat the eggs with a dash of pepper until thoroughly mixed; salt may not be needed as the bacon is already salty. Heat the butter in a 23-cm/9-in omelette pan or frying pan and when the butter foams, pour in the egg mixture. Stir briskly for 8 to 10 seconds with the flat of a fork until the eggs start to thicken. Quickly but carefully pull the cooked egg mixture from the sides of the pan to the centre, then tip the pan so that the uncooked egg mixture flows to the sides. Continue for 30 seconds to 1 minute until the eggs are almost set. Stir in the bacon mixture and continue stirring for a few seconds. Cook undisturbed for 15 to 20 seconds to brown the bottom of the omelette: it should be almost firm on top. Remove from the heat. Place a serving plate over the top of the omelette pan and invert the pan and plate. Slide the omelette back into the pan to brown the other side. Cut in wedges and serve hot or cold. **Serves 2**

How to make a folded omelette

Stir the egg mixture with the flat of a fork until thickened, shaking the pan to prevent sticking.

Fold a third of the omelette over the filling. Roll onto the plate so that the smooth underside of the omelette faces up.

Cheese Omelette

Omelette au Fromage

The outside of an omelette should be golden brown and the inside runny or firm, but never hard.

4 eggs
salt and freshly ground black pepper
25 g/1 oz butter
25 to 50 g/1 to 2 oz grated or finely diced Gruyère cheese

Use a fork to beat the eggs with salt and pepper in a small bowl until thoroughly mixed. Melt the butter in a 23-cm/9-in omelette pan or frying pan. When the butter foams and just starts to brown, pour in the eggs. Stir briskly over medium heat for 8 to 10 seconds with the flat of a fork until the eggs start to thicken. Quickly but carefully pull the cooked egg mixture from the sides of the pan to the centre, then tip the pan so that the uncooked mixture flows to the sides. Continue this for 30 seconds to 1 minute until the egg is cooked to taste. Cook undisturbed for 10 to 15 seconds to brown the bottom of the omelette. Sprinkle with the cheese.

To fold the omelette, hold the pan in your left hand and tip it towards you. Give the pan a sharp tap with your right hand so that the edge of the omelette folds over. Alternatively use a fork to fold over the edge of the omelette near the handle. Half roll, half slide the omelette on to a serving plate so it lands on the plate folded in three, seam side down. Serve at once. **Serves 2**

Variations

Tomato Omelette (*Omelette aux Tomates*) Omit the cheese. Peel, seed and coarsely chop 2 tomatoes. Melt 25 g/1 oz butter in a small frying pan. Stir in 1 finely chopped shallot, 1 crushed garlic clove (optional), the tomatoes and 1 teaspoon chopped mixed fresh herbs such as thyme, basil or parsley. Add salt and pepper to taste. Sauté gently, stirring occasionally until the mixture is thick and the liquid has evaporated. Keep hot and spoon into the omelette just before folding.

Mushroom Omelette (*Omelette aux Champignons*) Omit the cheese. Melt 25 g/1 oz butter in a small saucepan and use to sauté 100 g/4 oz sliced mushrooms until tender. Stir in 2 teaspoons of flour and 3 to 4 tablespoons white veal stock, chicken stock (both page 19) or milk. Cook for 2 to 3 minutes, stirring constantly, then stir in 2 to 3 tablespoons single cream, lemon juice and salt and pepper to taste. Keep the mixture hot and spoon into the omelette just before folding.

Sauces

Most cooks would agree that sauces are the greatest challenge of French cuisine. There are five basic sauces that form a logical structure: white sauce, velouté, brown sauce, Hollandaise and Mayonnaise. From these five, hundreds of other classic sauces can be developed.

When making any of them, there are three things to remember. First, the ingredients must be combined properly so they do not form lumps or separate. Second, the sauce must be the right consistency, neither too thick nor too runny. And third, the seasoning is vital.

Sauces can be divided into two types: flour-based sauces and emulsified sauces.

Flour-Based Sauces

Basic white sauce, velouté and basic brown sauce are all defined as *flour-based*, because they are thickened either with flour (for white and velouté) or with potato (for brown). In white and velouté sauces the flour is first cooked with melted butter to form a *roux*, then milk is added to make white sauce, or stock to make velouté sauce. For brown sauce, cornflour is mixed with a little liquid to form a thin paste and whisked into the remaining stock.

For a smooth texture, all of these sauces must be whisked continuously as they come to a boil. After that they should be stirred now and again to prevent sticking during cooking.

Cooking time for flour-based sauces depends on their consistency. If a sauce is thin, both in consistency and flavour, it must be boiled for 15 minutes or even half an hour so it evaporates and becomes thicker and more concentrated. This process is called *reduction* and applies most often to sauces based on stock, as milk scorches easily during long cooking. In any case, all flour-based sauces must be cooked at least 3 minutes to get rid of any taste of uncooked flour.

Emulsified Sauces

Emulsified sauces are more tricky than flour-based ones because their ingredients combine properly only at certain temperatures. The hot emulsified sauces, Hollandaise and Béarnaise, that are made with egg yolks and butter, should never be more than warm. Their cold cousin, Mayonnaise, which is based on egg yolks and oil, should be cool but not chilled.

Add the butter or oil to the egg yolks slowly, particularly at first when the emulsion is forming. Constant whisking is essential to prevent *curdling*, when fat separates from the egg yolks, giving a granular appearance. You'll know if a sauce is curdling because the consistency will change suddenly, becoming thin, with oily drops on the surface. If this happens, immediately stop adding the butter or oil and whisk furiously. Most sauces can be rescued even if they do curdle. For methods, see recipes.

Thickness and Seasoning

For most uses, the right thickness for a sauce is *coating consistency*. A sauce should never be so thick that you cannot see the shape and colour of the food it covers. On the other hand, too thin a sauce is unpleasantly watery. For how to judge the right consistency, see page 12.

Brown and velouté sauces are often served when they have the consistency of thin cream, particularly if they accompany roast or grilled meats instead of gravy. White sauce should always have body, and when used as a base for soufflés or croquettes or to coat foods for browning in the oven, it should be quite thick. If in doubt, make a sauce too thick as it can easily be diluted.

Careful seasoning of sauces is critical. Add seasoning at the beginning of cooking and taste often, adding salt and pepper little by little. The flavour of a finished sauce should be well-balanced: its role is to highlight but never to overwhelm.

Basic White Sauce

(Illustrated on page 71)

250 ml/8 fl oz	350 ml/12 fl oz		475 ml/16 fl oz	600 ml/1 pint
250 ml/8 fl oz	350 ml/12 fl oz	**milk**	475 ml/16 fl oz	600 ml/1 pint
1	1	**slices onion (optional)**	2	2
1	1	**bay leaf (optional)**	1	1
6	9	**peppercorns (optional)**	12	18
to taste	to taste	**salt & white pepper**	to taste	to taste
pinch	pinch	**nutmeg**	pinch	pinch
		Thick Sauce		
25 g/1 oz	40 g/1½ oz	**butter**	50 g/2 oz	75 g/3 oz
2 tablespoons	3 tablespoons	**flour**	40 g/1½ oz	50 g/2 oz
		Medium (coating) Sauce		
20 g/¾ oz	25 g/1 oz	**butter**	40 g/1½ oz	50 g/2 oz
6 teaspoons	2 tablespoons	**flour**	3 tablespoons	40 g/1½ oz
		Thin (pouring) Sauce		
15 g/½ oz	20 g/¾ oz	**butter**	25 g/1 oz	40 g/1½ oz
1 tablespoon	6 teaspoons	**flour**	2 tablespoons	3 tablespoons

Scald the milk by bringing it just to the boil. Add the onion, bayleaf and peppercorns, if using, cover and allow to stand for 5 to 10 minutes. Melt the butter in a medium-sized heavy saucepan and whisk in the flour. Cook over a low heat, whisking continuously for 1 to 2 minutes until foaming but not brown. Cool and strain the hot milk onto the butter mixture, whisking continuously. Bring the sauce to the boil still whisking, remove from heat and rub the surface with butter to prevent a skin forming. Basic White Sauce can be made 2 to 3 days ahead, covered and refrigerated or frozen.

Cream Sauce To 250 ml/8 fl oz medium white sauce, add 3 tablespoons single cream. Simmer until sauce is desired consistency then season to taste with salt and pepper.

Cheese Sauce

Sauce Mornay

Classic French cheese sauce goes well with eggs, fish, poultry, white meats and vegetables.

thin basic white sauce (page 69) made with
250 ml/8 fl oz milk
1 egg yolk
25 g/1 oz grated Gruyère *or* 1–2 rounded tablespoons grated Parmesan cheese or a combination of the two
salt and white pepper to taste
1 teaspoon French mustard (optional)

Prepare the white sauce and remove from the heat. Beat the egg yolk and cheese into the hot sauce and season to taste with salt and white pepper. **Makes 300 ml/½ pint**

Basic Brown Sauce

Fond de Veau Lié

(Illustrated on page 71)
Use as a base for Brown Mushroom Sauce, Madeira Sauce and Piquant Sauce.

750 ml / 1¼ pints brown veal stock (page 18)
1½ tablespoons cornflour
3 tablespoons Madeira or water
salt and pepper

If your stock does not have enough flavour reduce 1 litre / 1¾ pints to 750 ml / 1¼ pints to concentrate the flavour. Bring the stock to the boil. In a cup or small bowl mix the cornflour with the Madeira or water to make a paste. Gradually whisk the paste into the hot stock. Bring the sauce back to the boil, whisking constantly, then simmer until thick enough to coat the back of a spoon. Season to taste with salt and pepper. Strain through a fine strainer. Basic brown sauce can be made 4 days ahead, covered and refrigerated or frozen. **Makes 750 ml / 1¼ pints**

Mustard-flavoured Brown Sauce

Sauce Robert

This classic sauce is traditionally served with pork chops.

15 g / ½ oz butter
½ onion, finely chopped
175 ml / 6 fl oz white wine
3 tablespoons white wine vinegar
475 ml / 16 fl oz basic brown sauce (page 70)
2 tablespoons French mustard
salt and pepper

Melt the butter in a medium saucepan. Stir in the onion and sauté until soft but not brown. Pour in the wine and vinegar and boil until the liquid is reduced to 3 tablespoons. Stir in the brown sauce and bring to the boil. Remove from the heat and stir in the mustard. Season to taste with salt and pepper. Mustard-flavoured brown sauce can be made 4 days ahead, covered and refrigerated or frozen. **Makes 600 ml / 1 pint**

Brown Mushroom Sauce

Sauce Chasseur

This sauce goes well with all kinds of meat, particularly chicken or rabbit.

50 g / 2 oz butter
2 shallots, finely chopped
100 g / 4 oz mushrooms, thinly sliced
300 ml / ½ pint white wine
300 ml / ½ pint basic brown sauce (page 70)
300 ml / ½ pint tomato sauce (page 73) *or* 2 tablespoons concentrated tomato purée
1 tablespoon finely chopped parsley
2 teaspoons finely chopped fresh tarragon *or* ½ teaspoon dried tarragon
salt and pepper

Melt 25 g / 1 oz of the butter in a saucepan. Cut the remaining butter into pieces and set aside. Stir the shallots into the melted butter and sauté until soft but not brown. Stir in the mushrooms and cook over medium heat for 2–3 minutes until tender. Pour in the wine and boil until the liquid is reduced to about 4 tablespoons. Stir in the brown sauce and tomato sauce or tomato purée. Bring to the boil, stirring constantly. Remove immediately from the heat and whisk in the pieces of butter, the parsley and tarragon. Season lightly with salt and pepper. The sauce should not be boiled after the last addition of butter.

Brown Mushroom Sauce can be made 2 to 3 days ahead covered and refrigerated. It can be frozen before the last addition of butter. Add the butter to the re-heated sauce just before serving.
Makes 750 ml / 1¼ pints

From top to bottom **Basic White Sauce (previous page); Basic Brown Sauce (above); White Butter Sauce (page 75).**

Madeira Sauce

Sauce Madère

Excellent with beef fillet, veal, ham and offal such as liver.

5 tablespoons Madeira
600 ml/1 pint basic brown sauce (page 70)
salt and pepper

Combine 3 tablespoons of the Madeira and the basic brown sauce in a medium-sized saucepan. Simmer for 8 to 10 minutes. Stir in the remaining Madeira and bring the sauce just to the boil. Season lightly with salt and pepper. Madeira sauce can be made 4 days ahead, covered and refrigerated or frozen.
Makes 600 ml/1 pint

Piquant Sauce

Sauce Piquant

An enhancing sauce for pork, boiled beef and grilled chicken.

125 ml/4 fl oz white wine
125 ml/4 fl oz white wine vinegar
2 shallots, finely chopped
475 ml/16 fl oz basic brown sauce (page 70)
3 gherkins, coarsely chopped
1 tablespoon finely chopped parsley
2 teaspoons finely chopped fresh tarragon *or* ½ teaspoon dried tarragon
2 teaspoons finely chopped fresh chervil *or* ½ teaspoon dried chervil
salt and pepper

Combine the wine, vinegar and shallots in a medium-sized saucepan. Boil until the liquid is reduced to 1 tablespoon. Stir in the basic brown sauce and simmer for a further 5 minutes. Just before serving stir in the gherkins, parsley, tarragon and chervil and season to taste with salt and pepper. Piquant Sauce can be made 4 days ahead, covered and refrigerated or frozen.
Makes 475 ml/16 fl oz

Velouté Sauce

Sauce Velouté

This is one of the five basic sauces. Cream is usually added if the sauce is to be served with veal, poultry or fish.

300 ml/½ pint white veal stock, chicken stock (both page 19) or fish stock (page 20)
20 g/¾ oz butter
6 teaspoons plain flour
salt and white pepper

If your stock does not have a strong enough flavour reduce 600 ml/1 pint by rapid boiling to 300 ml/½ pint to concentrate the flavour.

Bring the stock to the boil. Melt the butter in a heavy-based saucepan and whisk in the flour. Cook over low heat for 1 to 2 minutes until the mixture is foaming but not brown. Cool slightly, then gradually whisk in the hot stock. Bring the sauce to the boil, whisking continuously. Season lightly as the flavour will concentrate as the sauce simmers. Reduce the heat and simmer for 5 to 10 minutes, skimming and whisking occasionally, until the sauce has reached the desired consistency. Taste and adjust the seasoning. Velouté sauce can be made 2 to 3 days ahead, covered and refrigerated or frozen. **Makes 300 ml/½ pint**

Variation

Creamy Velouté (*Velouté à la Crème*) Gradually stir 2 to 3 tablespoons double cream into the simmering sauce.

Sauce Suprème (*Sauce Suprème*) Add 25 g/1 oz chopped mushroom stalks to the butter mixture with the stock. After simmering to the desired consistency strain the sauce. Gradually stir in 3 tablespoons double cream. Return to the heat and simmer to reduce again if desired. Remove from the heat and season lightly with salt and white pepper. Stir in 15 g/½ oz butter in small pieces until melted. Sauce Suprème can be made 2 to 3 days ahead and refrigerated. It can be frozen before the butter is added. Add butter to reheated sauce just before serving.

Tomato Sauce

Sauce Tomate

Enjoy this sauce with veal, poultry, eggs, fish and pasta.

25 g/1 oz butter
1 onion, chopped
15 g/½ oz plain flour
450 ml/¾ pint stock or stock mixed with juice from the canned tomatoes
1 (793-g/1 lb 12-oz) can tomatoes, drained and chopped *or* 1 kg/2 lb fresh tomatoes, peeled and quartered
1 clove garlic, crushed
1 bouquet garni
1 teaspoon sugar
salt and pepper
2 tablespoons concentrated tomato purée

Melt the butter in a medium-sized saucepan and stir in the onion. Sauté until soft but not browned. Remove from the heat and stir in the flour. Pour in the stock and bring to the boil, stirring occasionally. Stir in the tomatoes, garlic, bouquet garni, sugar, salt and pepper and simmer uncovered, stirring occasionally, for 30–40 minutes for canned tomatoes and 45 minutes for fresh tomatoes or until the tomatoes are softened and the sauce is slightly thickened. Press the sauce through a sieve then return to a clean saucepan. Simmer until thick enough to coat the back of a spoon. If fresh tomatoes have been used, add the tomato purée to darken the colour. Taste and adjust the seasoning. **Makes 300 ml/½ pint**

Mayonnaise

Mayonnaise

Vary the flavour by substituting lemon juice for the vinegar and olive oil for some of the vegetable oil.

2 egg yolks
2 tablespoons white wine vinegar *or* 1 tablespoon lemon juice
1–2 teaspoons dry or French mustard (optional)
salt and white pepper
300 ml/½ pint vegetable, sunflower or soya oil

All the ingredients must be at room temperature before starting; if the egg yolks are too cold the mixture will not emulsify. On a cold day, warm the bowl and whisk in hot water.

In a small bowl beat until thick the egg yolks with half the vinegar or lemon juice, 1 teaspoon of the mustard and salt and pepper to taste. Add the oil drop by drop, whisking continuously. If the oil is added too fast the mixture will curdle. After 2 tablespoons of oil have been added the mixture should be very thick. The remaining oil can then be added in a thin stream. When all the oil has been added, flavour to taste with the remaining vinegar or lemon juice, mustard, salt and pepper. If desired, thin the mayonnaise with a little warm water. Store, covered, at room temperature.

Mayonnaise can be made 2 to 3 days ahead, covered and refrigerated. If it is chilled, bring it to room temperature before stirring or it may curdle.
Makes 300 ml/½ pint

Variations

Green Mayonnaise (*Mayonnaise Verte*) Boil 450 ml/¾ pint water in a medium saucepan. Add 6 spinach leaves, 15 g/½ oz parsley sprigs and 2 tablespoons fresh tarragon or chervil leaves and boil for 3 minutes. Remove, and rinse with cold water. Drain thoroughly and purée into 300 ml/½ pint mayonnaise. Season to taste with salt and pepper. Serve with fish, eggs and vegetables.

Rémoulade Sauce (*Sauce Rémoulade*) Stir 1 teaspoon French mustard, 2 tablespoons chopped capers, 3 tablespoons chopped gherkins, 1 tablespoon chopped parsley, 2 teaspoons chopped fresh chervil or ½ teaspoon dried chervil, 2 teaspoons chopped fresh tarragon or ½ teaspoon dried tarragon and ½ teaspoon anchovy paste or 1 teaspoon crushed anchovy fillets into 300 ml/½ pint mayonnaise. Season to taste with salt and pepper. Serve with fish, eggs and vegetables.

Béarnaise Sauce

Sauce Béarnaise

Serve this sauce with steak or with grilled or sautéed oily fish such as mackerel or herring.

175 g/6 oz butter
2 tablespoons vinegar
2 tablespoons white wine
10 peppercorns
3 shallots, finely chopped
1 tablespoon coarsely chopped fresh tarragon or tarragon leaves preserved in vinegar
3 egg yolks
salt and white pepper or cayenne
TO FINISH
1 tablespoon finely chopped fresh tarragon or tarragon leaves preserved in vinegar
1 tablespoon finely chopped chervil or parsley

Clarify the butter (page 12) and cool to lukewarm. In a small heavy saucepan combine the vinegar, wine, peppercorns, shallots and 1 tablespoon coarsely chopped tarragon. Boil until the liquid is reduced to 2 tablespoons then cool. Whisk in the egg yolks and salt and pepper or cayenne. Whisk for 30 seconds or until pale. Place the pan over a very low heat or in a water bath and whisk continuously until the mixture is creamy and thick enough for the whisk to leave a trail in the bottom of the pan. It should be slightly thicker than Hollandaise sauce. The pan should be hot but never too hot to touch. Remove from the heat and whisk in the clarified butter drop by drop; when the sauce starts to thicken it can be added in a thin stream. When all the butter has been added, strain the sauce.

Stir in the finely chopped tarragon leaves and chervil or parsley. Taste and adjust the seasoning; Béarnaise Sauce should have a peppery taste and is served warm rather than hot. It can be kept warm in a water bath for up to 1 hour but is best served immediately.
Makes 250 ml/8 fl oz

Remedies for Curdling

If Hollandaise or Béarnaise sauces curdle, it is almost always because they are too hot. Remove the curdled sauce from the heat and whisk in an ice-cube. If this is not successful, start the sauce again by whisking 1 egg yolk and 1 tablespoon water in a small saucepan over a low heat until creamy. Remove from the heat. Gradually whisk the curdled sauce drop by drop into the creamy egg yolk mixture. If the sauce is really badly curdled, it may have to be discarded.

Occasionally the sauces separate because they are undercooked and do not thicken properly. In this case whisk in 1 tablespoon of boiling water.

If mayonnaise curdles, beat in 1 tablespoon of boiling water. If this is not successful start again by beating a fresh egg yolk with salt and pepper. Whisk in the curdled mixture drop by drop. Or if mustard is used beat curdled mayonnaise into 1 teaspoon of French mustard.

Béarnaise Sauce

Far left Mix vinegar, wine, peppercorns, shallots and tarragon in a saucepan.

Centre The cooked mixture is thick enough when a whisk leaves a trail in the pan. If the mixture is overcooked, the eggs will become scrambled.

Left First whisk the clarified butter into the sauce drop by drop, then in a thin stream.

Hollandaise Sauce

Sauce Hollandaise

A favourite with eggs, vegetables and poached fish.

175 g/6 oz butter
2 tablespoons water
3 egg yolks
salt and white pepper
juice of about $\frac{1}{2}$ lemon
1 tablespoon lukewarm water (optional)

Clarify the butter (page 12) and cool to lukewarm. In a small heavy saucepan, whisk the water with the egg yolks and a little salt and pepper for about 30 seconds or until pale. Place the pan over very low heat or in a water bath and whisk constantly until the mixture is creamy and thick enough for the whisk to leave a trail in the base of the pan. The pan should be hot but never too hot to touch comfortably. Remove from heat and whisk in the clarified butter, a few drops at a time. Do not add the butter too fast or the sauce may curdle. When the sauce starts to thicken, butter can be added a little faster. After all the butter has been added stir in the salt, white pepper and lemon juice to taste. Hollandaise sauce is served warm, not hot. It can be kept warm in a water bath for up to 1 hour but is best served immediately. If the sauce is too thick, stir in 1 tablespoon lukewarm water just before serving.
Makes 250 ml/8 fl oz

White Butter Sauce

Sauce Beurre Blanc

(Illustrated on page 71)
An extremely delicate sauce, thickened only with butter. Beurre Blanc is delicious with poached fish.

2 tablespoons white wine vinegar
2 shallots, very finely chopped
2 tablespoons dry white wine
1 tablespoon single cream
225 g/8 oz chilled butter cut in small pieces
salt and white pepper

In a small heavy saucepan, boil the vinegar and shallots until the liquid is reduced to 1 tablespoon. Add the wine and continue to boil for 5 minutes or until reduced again to 1 to 2 tablespoons. Stir in the cream and reduce again to 1 to 2 tablespoons. Place the pan over a very low heat and gradually whisk in the butter, piece by piece. The butter must be very cold to achieve a smooth, creamy sauce. Remove from the heat occasionally, whisking continuously so that the butter softens and thickens the sauce without melting. Season to taste with salt and pepper and serve immediately. The sauce can be kept warm in a water bath for a few minutes but the butter tends to melt and make the sauce oily. If the sauce does separate, it cannot be remedied.
Makes 250 ml/8 fl oz

Vegetables

A French dinner without vegetables is hard to imagine. As starters they provide a lively and versatile introduction to almost any main course. As accompaniments, vegetables contribute lightness and colour, while potatoes and rice with their more neutral flavours are the perfect background for rich meats and sauces. Vegetables often contribute vital flavouring for stocks and sauces but are not seen as they are strained out before serving.

How to Choose and Store Vegetables

Fresh vegetables are easy to recognise because they look good and are bright – coloured and firm with no brown spots or wilted leaves. Because freshness is the key to flavour, try to cook them as soon as possible. If they must be stored, keep greens and softer vegetables such as tomatoes or courgettes loosely covered in the bottom of the refrigerator. Do not leave them sealed in plastic or they will rot. Root vegetables particularly are best kept at room temperature, even if the kitchen is warm. Potatoes should never be chilled or they will go black.

How to Cook Vegetables

Green vegetables such as spinach, peas, beans, asparagus, cabbage and broccoli overcook very easily, losing taste and colour. They should be cooked as fast as possible over high heat in large quantities of boiling salted water. Leave the pan uncovered so the vegetables do not stew. Drain thoroughly so they do not 'weep' when served. Spinach retains so much water that it must be squeezed by handfuls to get rid of the excess. The French often dry their green vegetables still further by turning them in butter over low heat.

The cooking of root vegetables such as carrots, potatoes, turnips or onions should start in cold salted water to extract over-strong flavour. Cook in a covered pan, simmering rather than boiling. Root vegetables are not usually rinsed, but they must be drained well before serving.

Fleshy vegetables include tomatoes, mushrooms, peppers and aubergines as well as members of the squash family such as marrow and courgette. Rarely cooked in water, they are more often sautéed or baked.

For all vegetables only a rough guide can be given to cooking times because they vary enormously with the age and size of the vegetables and how tender you want them to be. For most recipes the vegetable should have lost its toughness but still be firm and, for a green vegetable, slightly crisp.

Getting Ahead

Few vegetables should be kept waiting because whether cooked or raw, their taste depends on freshness. However, cooked root vegetables can be stored covered in the refrigerator and reheated in butter the following day. Greens can have the same treatment, though their flavour will not be quite so lively. Potatoes taste stale if refrigerated after cooking – unless they are in a casserole such as Gratin of Potatoes in Cream. Fleshy vegetables are more accommodating, and most recipes using them are even improved if made a day or two ahead so the flavours have time to blend. If you have cooked vegetables left over, they are good made into a salad with a vinaigrette dressing or mayonnaise. For a hot dish convert them to a delicious gratin by coating the vegetable – or a mixture of vegetables – with a white sauce in a shallow baking dish. Sprinkle the top generously with grated cheese or breadcrumbs, dot with butter and bake until browned.

How to Serve Vegetables

The French like to serve fresh vegetables as simply as possible. They boil them in salted water, drain and reheat in butter. More mature vegetables may be puréed and laced with butter and cream to bring out the flavour. One excellent treatment for root vegetables is to glaze them by cooking gently with butter and a little sugar.

Artichokes Vinaigrette

Artichauts Vinaigrette

The classic summertime starter with a simple vinaigrette dressing.

4 large artichokes
salt and pepper
4 tablespoons wine vinegar
150 ml/¼ pint olive or vegetable oil
2 tablespoons chopped fresh herbs such as parsley, tarragon, chives or chervil

Break the stems from the artichokes to remove any tough fibres. Cut 2.5 cm/1 in off the top with a knife and snip off the sharp points of each leaf with scissors. Wash the artichokes well. In a large saucepan, bring to the boil enough salted water to cover the artichokes. Put the artichokes into boiling water and place a piece of greaseproof paper on the surface of the water to keep the artichokes submerged. Reduce the heat and simmer uncovered for 30 to 40 minutes until a leaf can easily be pulled out. Lift the artichokes from the water. If serving cold rinse the artichokes with cold water. Gently squeeze excess water from each artichoke and drain upside down for 5 minutes to prevent the artichokes becoming soggy.

Firmly grasp the tender, purple leaves in the centre of the artichoke and pull out in one piece to retain the cup shape. Scoop out the hairy choke with a teaspoon and discard.

To make the dressing: whisk the vinegar with the salt and pepper then beat in the oil a little at a time so the dressing emulsifies. Taste and adjust the seasoning, then whisk in the chopped herbs. Pour a little dressing into the cup in the centre of each artichoke and serve the rest separately. **Serves 4**

Green Peas with Lettuce and Onions

Petits Pois à la Française

The bigger the peas, the longer they need to cook, so cooking time can vary from 20 to 45 minutes.

1 small cos lettuce
450 g/1 lb fresh, shelled or frozen peas
6 to 8 spring onions, cut in 5-cm/2-in lengths
2 teaspoons sugar
25 to 50 g/1 to 2 oz butter
1 bouquet garni
150 ml/¼ pint water
salt and pepper
1 tablespoon flour (optional)

Shred the lettuce coarsely. Place all the ingredients except 25 g/1 oz of the butter and the flour in a heavy saucepan, cover and simmer over low heat for 20 to 45 minutes until the peas and spring onions are tender, shaking the pan occasionally to prevent sticking. Discard the bouquet garni. If the peas are a little dry, add the remaining butter in pieces, shaking the pan occasionally until the butter is melted and absorbed. If there is too much liquid in the peas, use a fork to mix the flour with the remaining butter and add this mixture to the peas in small pieces, shaking the pan over the heat until the liquid thickens slightly. Taste and adjust the seasoning and spoon into a serving dish. **Serves 4**

Carrot Purée

Purée de Carottes

The golden colour of carrot purée is a pretty addition to any main course.

675 g / $1\frac{1}{2}$ lb carrots, sliced
salt and pepper
3 tablespoons single cream
40 g / $1\frac{1}{2}$ oz butter
$\frac{1}{2}$ to 1 teaspoon granulated sugar (optional)

Put the carrots in a large saucepan and cover with water. Add a pinch of salt and boil for 8 to 12 minutes until the carrots are very tender. Drain well. Purée with the cream in a liquidiser or food processor. Melt the butter in a saucepan, add the carrot purée and heat over low heat. Season to taste with sugar, salt and pepper. If the purée is too runny, cook and stir until it thickens. **Serves 4**

Glazed Carrots

Carottes Vichy

Named after the town of Vichy, which is also famous for its mineral water.

450 g / 1 lb new carrots, trimmed, or large carrots, quartered or sliced
2 teaspoons sugar
25 g / 1 oz butter
$\frac{1}{2}$ teaspoon salt
1 tablespoon chopped fresh mint or parsley

Put the carrots in a shallow saucepan with the sugar, butter and salt and just cover with water. Bring to the boil, reduce the heat and simmer uncovered for 8 to 12 minutes for baby carrots or 15 to 20 minutes for large carrots until almost tender. Boil rapidly until all the liquid has evaporated to form a shiny glaze. Toward the end of cooking time, watch carefully so the sugar does not caramelise. Taste and adjust the seasoning. Just before serving add the chopped mint or parsley, toss and spoon into a serving dish. **Serves 4**

Carrot Purée

Add puréed cooked carrots to melted butter. The mixture should fall thickly from a spoon.

Use a rubber spatula to make decorative ripples on the surface of the finished puree.

Asparagus with Butter Sauce

Snap off the fibrous ends of the asparagus spears.

Arrange the asparagus in bundles and tie with string.

Asparagus with Butter Sauce

Asperges au Beurre

This is delicious served as a starter for a summer dinner party.

1 kg/2 lb fresh asparagus
SAUCE
225 g/8 oz butter
2 tablespoons water
juice of ½ lemon
salt and pepper

Choose asparagus spears of the same thickness so they cook evenly. Snap off the fibrous ends of the stems. Peel the lower part of the stem with a vegetable peeler. Tie the asparagus spears with string in four even-sized bundles.

Place the bundles in a large shallow saucepan of boiling salted water. The water should cover the asparagus and the bundles should not overlap. Cover and boil for 8 to 10 minutes until the stems are almost tender when pierced with a knife. Prepare the melted butter sauce following the instructions below. Drain the asparagus, transfer to a serving dish and remove the strings. Pour a little sauce over the asparagus and serve the remaining sauce separately.

Melted Butter Sauce

Cut the butter into small cubes. Combine the water, lemon juice, salt and pepper in a small non-aluminium saucepan over very low heat. Whisk in the butter piece by piece, removing the pan from the heat occasionally and whisking constantly so that the butter softens and thickens the sauce without melting. The base of the pan should never be more than warm. Taste for seasoning, adding more lemon juice if necessary. Serve immediately. Melted butter sauce can be kept warm for a few minutes by placing the pan in a container of lukewarm water, but the butter tends to melt and make the sauce oily. If the sauce does separate, it cannot be re-emulsified. **Serves 4**

Braised Cabbage

Choux Braisés

Cabbage cooked in this way is especially good with beef and pork.

1 medium head firm green cabbage, halved and cored
100 g/4 oz bacon, diced
1 onion, sliced
salt and pepper
3 tablespoons stock or water

Preheat the oven to moderate (180 C, 350 F, gas 4). Shred the cabbage. Dry-fry the bacon until brown in a flameproof casserole. Stir in the onion and sauté until the onion is golden brown. Add the shredded cabbage, salt and pepper and mix thoroughly. Pour in the stock. Cover and bake for 30 to 40 minutes until cabbage is very tender, stirring once or twice. Remove the lid towards the end of the cooking time if the cabbage mixture is very moist. Taste and adjust the seasoning. Serve hot. **Serves 4**

Braised Red Cabbage

Choux Rouges Braisés

A favourite recipe in the Ardennes region in northern France.

1 medium head red cabbage, halved and cored
25 g/1 oz butter
1 onion, sliced
1 tablespoon granulated sugar
1 tablespoon vinegar
150 ml/$\frac{1}{4}$ pint red wine
salt and pepper

Preheat the oven to moderate (180 C, 350 F, gas 4). Shred the cabbage. Heat the butter in a large flameproof casserole and stir in the onion. Sauté until soft but not browned. Add the sugar and cook, stirring constantly, until the sugar caramelises. Add the shredded cabbage and the vinegar and stir thoroughly. Add the red wine and season to taste with salt and pepper. Cover and bake for 45 to 55 minutes until the cabbage is very tender, stirring once or twice. Remove the lid towards the end of the cooking time if the cabbage is very moist. Taste for seasoning, adding a little more sugar or vinegar if necessary. Serve hot. **Serves 4**

Braised Chicory

Endives Braisées

Unlike many green vegetables, chicory is best when cooked until very soft.

4 to 6 heads chicory (about 675 g/1$\frac{1}{2}$ lb)
40 g/1$\frac{1}{2}$ oz butter
salt and pepper
1 teaspoon sugar
squeeze of lemon juice
2 tablespoons water
1 tablespoon chopped parsley

Preheat the oven to moderate (180 C, 350 F, gas 4). Discard any wilted leaves from the chicory and trim the stems. Do not wash them. Using a sharp knife, hollow the stems slightly to allow the chicory to cook more evenly. Thickly coat the bottom and sides of a shallow baking dish with butter. Place the chicory in the dish and sprinkle with salt, pepper, sugar, lemon juice and water. Press a piece of buttered foil over the chicory and cover with a lid. Cook for 50 to 60 minutes until the chicory cores are very tender. If the dish becomes dry during cooking, add a little more water. The chicory should brown lightly without burning. Sprinkle with parsley before serving. **Serves 4**

Sautéed Cucumbers

Concombres Sautés

A light and refreshing vegetable to serve with lamb or fish – especially salmon.

2 cucumbers
40 g/1$\frac{1}{2}$ oz butter
salt and pepper
1 tablespoon chopped fresh mint, dill or parsley

Peel the cucumbers, cut them in half lengthways and scoop out the seeds with a teaspoon. Slice each half once again lengthways, then cut into 5-cm/2-in sticks. Place the cucumber in a pan of boiling salted water. Boil for 4 to 5 minutes until almost tender, then drain.

Melt the butter in a large frying pan, add the cucumbers and sauté for 3 to 4 minutes until just tender. Do not overcook or they will be bitter. Remove from the heat. Add salt, pepper and mint, dill or parsley. Toss and transfer to a serving dish. **Serves 4**

Spinach Soufflé

Soufflé aux Épinards

'A soufflé,' say the French, 'is a bit of theatre' – the perfect opening for a grand dinner.

3 tablespoons dry breadcrumbs
350 g/12 oz fresh spinach
50 g/2 oz butter
15 g/½ oz flour
150 ml/¼ pint milk
150 ml/¼ pint cream
salt and pepper
pinch of nutmeg
4 egg yolks and 6 egg whites
25 g/1 oz Gruyère *or* 15 g/½ oz Parmesan cheese, grated

Generously butter a 1.4-litre/2½-pint soufflé dish, being sure the edge is greased well so the mixture won't stick. Sprinkle the buttered dish with 2 tablespoons bread-crumbs. Remove the stems from the spinach and wash the leaves thoroughly. Cook the spinach in plenty of boiling salted water for 5 minutes or until tender, stirring occasionally. Drain the cooked spinach, rinse with cold water and drain again. Squeeze by handfuls to extract as much water as possible. Finely chop the spinach with a knife; do not purée.

Melt half the butter in a saucepan. Add the spinach and stir over medium heat until dry. Melt the remaining butter in a small saucepan. Whisk in the flour and cook over a low heat, whisking constantly, until the mixture is foaming but not browned. Remove from the heat and whisk in the milk and cream. Season to taste with salt, pepper and nutmeg. Bring to the boil, whisking constantly. Reduce the heat and simmer for 3 to 5 minutes. Stir in the spinach and heat through thoroughly. Remove from the heat and beat the egg yolks into the hot mixture to thicken. Taste and adjust the seasoning; the mixture should be highly seasoned. Spinach Soufflé can be prepared to this point 3 to 4 hours ahead. Rub the surface of the mixture with butter to prevent a skin forming, cover and refrigerate.

Thirty minutes before serving, preheat the oven to hot (220 C, 425 F, gas 7). Whip the egg whites until stiff. Heat the spinach mixture over low heat, whisking constantly, until it is hot to the touch. Remove from the heat and thoroughly mix in about a quarter of the stiff egg whites. Add this mixture with most of the cheese to the remaining egg whites. Fold lightly together. Spoon into the prepared soufflé dish and sprinkle with a mixture of remaining breadcrumbs and cheese. Bake for 12 to 15 minutes until the soufflé is risen and brown. Serve immediately. **Serves 4**

Spinach Purée

Purée d'Épinards

Use as an accompaniment alongside carrot purée or mashed potatoes for an attractive colour contrast.

675 g/1½ lb fresh spinach
25 g/1 oz butter
1 tablespoon flour
150 ml/¼ pt single cream or milk
salt and pepper
pinch of nutmeg

Remove the stems from the spinach and wash the leaves thoroughly. Plunge the spinach into freshly boiled, lightly salted water in a large saucepan. Boil for 5 minutes or until tender, stirring occasionally. Drain the cooked spinach, rinse with cold water and drain again. Squeeze by handfuls to extract as much water as possible then set aside.

Melt the butter in a small saucepan and whisk in the flour. Cook over low heat, whisking constantly, until the mixture foams but doesn't brown. Remove from the heat and whisk in the cream or milk. Bring to the boil, whisking constantly. Season to taste with salt, pepper and nutmeg. Reduce the heat and simmer for 3 to 5 minutes. Purée the spinach with the cream sauce in a liquidiser or food processor, in batches if necessary. Pour into a heavy saucepan and heat for 2 to 3 minutes over medium heat. The purée should be soft enough to fall from the spoon without being soupy. Taste and adjust the seasoning. **Serves 4**

Variation

Light Spinach Purée (*Purée Légère d'Épinards*) Omit the cream sauce. Purée the cooked spinach with 150 ml/¼ pint double cream in a liquidiser or food processor. Melt 15 g/½ oz butter in a medium saucepan, add the spinach purée and heat as directed above.

Ratatouille

Ratatouille

This vegetable stew originated in Provence and can be served as a starter or an accompaniment.

1 medium aubergine, halved, cut in 1-cm/½-in slices
225 g/8 oz small courgettes, sliced
4 tablespoons olive oil
2 medium-sized onions, thinly sliced
4 large tomatoes, peeled, seeded and chopped *or* 1 (396-g/14-oz) can tomatoes, drained and chopped
2 red or green peppers, cored, seeded and sliced
2 cloves garlic, crushed
1 teaspoon dried basil
½ teaspoon dried thyme
½ teaspoon ground coriander
pinch of crushed aniseed
salt and pepper
1 tablespoon chopped parsley

Sprinkle the slices of aubergine and courgette with salt and leave to stand for 30 minutes. Drain, rinse with cold water and dry on absorbent kitchen paper. Heat 2 tablespoons of the oil in a large casserole. Add the onions and sauté until soft but not browned. Layer the onions, aubergine, courgettes, tomatoes and peppers in a large flameproof casserole. Mix the garlic, basil, thyme, coriander, aniseed, salt and pepper together and sprinkle over the casserole. Mix the vegetables thoroughly, then spoon the remaining 2 tablespoons olive oil over the vegetables. Cover the casserole and simmer over medium heat for 30 to 40 minutes until the vegetables are tender. Do not overcook. If the mixture is too moist remove the lid for the last 10 minutes of cooking time. Taste and adjust the seasoning.

Ratatouille can be prepared up to 3 days ahead, but it should be slightly underdone to allow for reheating. If preparing ahead, cover and refrigerate. Serve hot or cold. Reheat chilled Ratatouille over medium heat. Stir in the chopped parsley just before serving. **Serves 4**

Potatoes Anna

Pommes Anna

A golden brown cake of thinly sliced potatoes.

675 g/1½ lb medium-sized potatoes, peeled
2 tablespoons vegetable oil
75 g/3 oz butter
salt and pepper

Preheat the oven to moderately hot (200 C, 400 F, gas 6). Slice the potatoes as thinly as possible. Do not soak in water as this removes the starch needed to hold the slices together. Heat the vegetable oil and 25 g/1 oz of the butter in an 18 to 20-cm/7 to 8-in frying pan with an ovenproof handle, or shallow ovenproof casserole, tipping it to coat the sides with fat. Do not let the butter brown. Remove from the heat and arrange a layer of potato slices overlapping in a spiral pattern in the bottom of the frying pan or casserole. When the potatoes are unmoulded, the spiral design will show on the top. Add another layer of potatoes – these don't need to be arranged in a pattern. Sprinkle lightly with salt and pepper and dot with butter. Continue adding layers of potatoes with seasoning and butter until all the potatoes are used and the pan is full. Cook over medium heat for 10 to 15 minutes until the potatoes are browned on the bottom. To test, slide a metal spatula down the side of the potato cake and lift slightly – you should be able to smell the browned butter. For a crisp bottom crust, leave uncovered; for a softer potato cake, cover with foil.

Place the frying pan in the centre of the oven. Cook for 25 to 30 minutes, pressing the potatoes occasionally with a spatula, until tender when tested with a skewer. To serve, loosen the edge of the potato cake with a spatula. Place a plate over the frying pan or casserole and invert so the potato cake falls on to the platter. **Serves 4**

Potatoes Anna (above).

Creamed Potatoes

Purée de Pommes de Terre

Good creamed potatoes should be smooth, light and fluffy.

1 kg/2 lb potatoes, peeled
125 to 150 ml/4 to 5 fl oz milk
40 g/$1\frac{1}{2}$ oz butter
salt and white pepper
pinch of nutmeg

Cut the potatoes into even-sized pieces. Put the potatoes in a large saucepan and cover with cold water. Add salt to taste, cover and bring to the boil. Simmer for 15 to 20 minutes until tender; the potatoes should be quite soft. In a small saucepan, scald the milk by bringing it just to the boil. Drain the potatoes and press through a sieve or mash in the pan with a potato masher. Beat in the butter, 125 ml/4 fl oz of the hot milk and salt, white pepper and nutmeg to taste. Continue beating over low heat until the purée is light and fluffy. The heat should cause the grains of starch in the potatoes to expand. If necessary, add more milk to make a soft purée that just falls from the spoon. Taste and adjust the seasoning. Serve hot. **Serves 4**

Duchess Potatoes

Pommes Duchesse

The potatoes contain egg yolks, making them thick enough for piping rosettes or a decorative border.

675 g/$1\frac{1}{2}$ lb potatoes, peeled
40 g/$1\frac{1}{2}$ oz butter
salt and white pepper
pinch of nutmeg
3 egg yolks

Cut the potatoes into equal-sized pieces. Place in a large saucepan and cover with cold water. Add a pinch of salt, cover the pan and bring to the boil. Simmer for 15 to 20 minutes until tender. The potatoes should be quite soft. Drain them, return the potatoes to the pan and heat very gently, shaking occasionally until dry. Press the hot potatoes through a sieve. Return to the pan. Beat in the butter, salt, white pepper and nutmeg to taste. Continue beating over low heat until the potatoes are light and fluffy. Remove from the heat and beat in the egg yolks. Taste and adjust the seasoning. The purée should hold its shape well and stick to a spoon.

Grease a baking sheet or, if piping a potato border, the edge of a heatproof dish. Spoon the purée into a piping bag fitted with a medium star-shaped vegetable nozzle and pipe large rosettes, figures of eight or small mounds of potato on the baking sheet or a border around the serving dish. Duchess potatoes can be piped several hours ahead, covered and kept at room temperature. Just before serving, heat the grill until hot. Grill for 5 to 10 minutes until browned. Alternatively bake in a very hot oven (230 C, 450 F, gas 8) for the same length of time. **Serves 4**

Gratin of Potatoes in Cream

Gratin Dauphinois

A rich version of scalloped potatoes. Curdling is prevented by parboiling the potatoes in milk.

1 clove garlic, halved
675 g/$1\frac{1}{2}$ lb potatoes, peeled
450 ml/$\frac{3}{4}$ pint milk
450 ml/$\frac{3}{4}$ pint single cream
salt and pepper
pinch of nutmeg
50 g/2 oz Gruyère cheese, grated
15 g/$\frac{1}{2}$ oz butter

Rub a 1-litre/$1\frac{3}{4}$-pint shallow flameproof dish with garlic, then butter generously. Slice the potatoes about 5 mm/$\frac{1}{4}$ in thick. Do not soak in water as this removes the starch needed to hold the slices together. Bring the milk to the boil in a large saucepan, add the potato slices and cook for 5 to 10 minutes until partly tender. Drain and discard the milk or use for soup. Return the potatoes to the saucepan. Add the cream, salt, pepper and nutmeg. Bring to the boil, reduce the heat and simmer for 10 to 15 minutes until the potatoes are tender but not falling apart. The mixture should be very moist. Taste and adjust the seasoning. Spoon into the prepared baking dish. Sprinkle with cheese and dot with butter. Place the dish under a hot grill and cook until golden brown. **Serves 4–6**

Cauliflower with Egg and Breadcrumbs

Choufleur à la Polonaise

Be careful not to overcook cauliflower – it should remain slightly crisp.

1 medium cauliflower
40 g / 1½ oz butter
15 g / ½ oz fresh breadcrumbs
salt and pepper
1 hard-boiled egg, finely chopped
1 tablespoon chopped parsley

Divide the cauliflower into florets, discarding the stem. Cook in boiling salted water for 8 to 10 minutes until just tender. Drain, rinse with cold water and drain again. Arrange the florets on a warmed serving dish. Cover with foil and keep warm. Melt the butter in a small frying pan. Fry the breadcrumbs in butter until golden brown, stirring constantly. Add the salt and pepper. Immediately sprinkle the breadcrumbs over the cauliflower. Top with hard-boiled egg and parsley and serve hot. **Serves 4**

Leek Gratin

Poireaux au Gratin

Most vegetables can be made into a gratin which can be served as a starter or with a main course.

450 g / 1 lb medium leeks
Medium-thick basic white sauce made with
475 ml / 16 fl oz milk
50 g / 2 oz Gruyère or 25 g / 1 oz Parmesan cheese, grated

Trim the leeks, discarding the green tops. Quarter the leeks lengthwise, cutting almost to the root. Wash very thoroughly. Put the leeks in a medium saucepan with enough boiling salted water to cover. Boil for 12 to 15 minutes until tender. Drain, rinse with cold water and drain again. Grease a 2-litre/3½-pint shallow baking dish. Spoon a thin coat of white sauce over the bottom of the prepared baking dish. Cut the leeks into 8-cm/3-in lengths and arrange over the white sauce. Coat with the remaining sauce and sprinkle with the cheese. Bake the gratin in a hot oven (220 C, 425 F, gas 7) for 10 to 15 minutes until bubbling and browned. **Serves 4**

Rice Pilaf

Riz Pilaf

If you use stock instead of water, the pilaf will have a richer flavour.

25 g / 1 oz butter
1 onion, finely chopped
275 g / 10 oz long-grain rice
750 ml / 1¼ pints chicken stock (page 19) or water
1 bouquet garni
salt and pepper

Preheat the oven to moderate (180 C, 350 F, gas 4). Melt the butter in a medium-sized heavy ovenproof casserole with a tight-fitting lid. Add the onion and sauté gently until soft but not browned. Add the rice and sauté for a further 2 minutes, stirring constantly, until the butter is absorbed and the rice grains are transparent. Add the chicken stock or water, bouquet garni and salt and pepper to taste. Press a piece of buttered foil over the rice and cover with a lid. Bring to the boil, place in the oven and cook for 18 minutes. If the liquid has evaporated but the rice is not cooked, add more liquid and cook for a few more minutes until tender. Remove from the oven and leave to stand covered for 10 minutes. Remove the lid and discard the bouquet garni. Fluff up the rice with a fork. Taste and adjust the seasoning. Serve straight from the casserole. **Serves 5–6**

Variation

Rice Pilaff with Mushrooms Sauté 100 g/4 oz lean bacon, diced, with the onion and use white veal stock (page 18) *or* brown beef stock (page 19) instead of chicken stock. Add 100 g/4 oz lightly sautéed mushrooms to the rice with the stock and proceed as above.

Salads and Dressings

A simple lettuce salad tossed in oil and vinegar is most popular in France. It is seldom varied except to use seasonal greens. Many French first course salads are scarcely more complicated. They are based on one raw or cooked vegetable, mixed or sprinkled with a simple dressing. For instance, in summer the ripest tomatoes are sliced and marinated in vinaigrette with a little chopped shallot and fresh mixed herbs. Sliced cucumber is mixed with yogurt and topped with chives. Crudités, a mixture of three or four fresh vegetables, each of different colour and texture, is a standard restaurant starter.

However, more elaborate salads are rapidly becoming popular as the opening to a meal. They vary from classics like Niçoise Salad to imaginative combinations that mix fish with meat and a few nuts for texture.

How to Prepare Salads

There is nothing to camouflage salad ingredients, so they must be the best. In mixed salads, look for colour contrast like that in Rice Salad with peppers, carrots, tomatoes and peas against the white background of rice. Texture is important too, the aim being the balance of soft and crisp. With this in mind, it is best to shred raw vegetables such as carrots or cabbage in fine pieces, or cut them in julienne strips so you don't have to bite hard lumps. Blanch strong ingredients such as peppers so they don't dominate a salad, but be sure to leave them crisp, otherwise they will lack texture and flavour. Always drain and dry fresh and cooked vegetables thoroughly so they don't dilute the dressing.

The dressing for a salad is at least as important as the ingredients. Again, the French like to keep it simple. Vinaigrette, the most common dressing, is based on only four ingredients: oil, vinegar, salt and pepper. Its character is changed to a startling extent not only by the oil, which can vary from neutral vegetable oil to fruity olive or walnut oil, but also by the vinegar. Most popular is a mild red or white wine vinegar, but you could try a herb vinegar. Alternatively use lemon juice for a truly Mediterranean flavour. Mustard, finely chopped herbs, shallots, garlic or capers are also possible additions, but the French like to use them mainly with strongly flavoured ingredients like cooked meats and root vegetables.

Mayonnaise is popular but less versatile than vinaigrette as a dressing. It can overwhelm delicate flavours and it would mask the vivid colour in a salad using red cabbage for instance. So mayonnaise is usually reserved for dry foods such as cooked poultry or fish and for root vegetables. It is never used in a green salad.

How to Serve Salads

Salad ingredients should be mixed gently but thoroughly with dressing. Robust ingredients such as root vegetables and rice benefit from marinating in the dressing for at least one hour to blend the flavours. On the other hand green vegetables should remain crisp and must be mixed with dressing just before serving. If they sit for even half an hour in the dressing, the leaves will become soggy. Exceptions are curly endive and dandelion greens which will lose some of their toughness if dressed up to an hour ahead of time. Add only enough dressing to flavour and moisten the salad. Always taste a salad after mixing as some ingredients absorb more seasoning than you might expect.

Raw Vegetable Salad **(page 89)**

Cucumber Salad

Salade de Concombres

This salad is also very good with dill or mint instead of the chives.

1 large cucumber, peeled and thinly sliced
salt
150 ml/¼ pint natural yogurt
2 tablespoons chopped fresh chives
salt and pepper

Sprinkle the cucumber with salt and leave to stand for 30 minutes to draw out any bitter juices. Rinse with cold water and drain thoroughly on absorbent kitchen paper. In a bowl, mix the cucumber with the yogurt and 1 tablespoon chives. Season to taste with salt and black pepper. Place in a serving dish and sprinkle with the remaining chives. Cover and refrigerate for 2 to 4 hours. **Serves 4**

Potatoes Vinaigrette

Pommes de Terre Vinaigrette

French potato salad is delicious with hot sausage.

675 g/1½ lb waxy-textured potatoes, washed but unpeeled
triple quantity vinaigrette (page 91) made with mustard
salt and pepper
1 tablespoon finely chopped fresh chives

Place the potatoes in a large saucepan with enough salted water to cover. Cover and bring to the boil. Simmer for 15 to 20 minutes until just tender. Drain the potatoes and cool slightly. Peel and cut into pieces. Place in a serving dish and pour the vinaigrette over the potatoes while they are still warm. Mix gently and season to taste with salt and pepper. Cover and leave to stand for up to 2 hours at room temperature. Gently stir in chives just before serving. **Serves 4**

Green Salad

Salade Verte

To give just a hint of flavour, rub a cut clove of garlic around the salad bowl before adding the greens.

450 g/1 lb lettuce or other salad greens such as watercress, chicory, spinach or dandelion leaves
1 quantity vinaigrette dressing (above)
salt and pepper (optional)

Carefully wash the salad greens. Tear, do not cut, into pieces and dry thoroughly. Just before serving toss the salad in the dressing. Taste for seasoning, adding extra salt and pepper, if desired. Serve immediately because most greens will soften rapidly and become soggy once they are dressed. **Serves 4–6**

Cooked Vegetable Salad

Macédoine de Légumes

Warm vegetables will absorb the dressing more easily than cold ones

2 medium-sized carrots, diced
½ celeriac *or* 225 g/8 oz turnip, diced
100 g/4 oz shelled peas
100 g/4 oz French beans, cut in 1-cm/½-in lengths
1 quantity vinaigrette (page 91)
4–6 tablespoons mayonnaise (page 73)
salt and pepper

Put the carrots, celeriac or turnip in a pan and cover generously with cold salted water. Bring to the boil and cook for 10 to 12 minutes until just tender. Drain thoroughly. In another saucepan boil enough salted water to cover both the peas and beans. Add the peas and beans and boil for 5 to 8 minutes until just tender. Drain, rinse with cold water and drain thoroughly.

Mix the vinaigrette with the warm vegetables. When cool, mix the vegetables with enough mayonnaise to coat lightly, being careful not to add too much mayonnaise or the salad will be heavy. Season to taste with salt and pepper. Cover and leave to stand for 1 to 2 hours at room temperature to blend the flavours. **Serves 4**

Raw Vegetable Salad

Crudités

(Illustrated on page 86)
There are countless variations on this fresh appetizer which can be made according to the seasons.

Celeriac with Mayonnaise (page 90)
Cucumber Salad (page 88)
Tomato Salad (page 91)

Prepare the Celeriac with Mayonnaise, Cucumber Salad and Tomato Salad according to the recipes. Arrange the salads in separate mounds on a long or circular serving dish. **Serves 6–8**

Variations

One or more of the following salads can be added to the platter or substituted for any of the above salads.

Beetroot Salad (*Salade de Betteraves*) Mix 1 quantity vinaigrette, page 91, with 225 g/8 oz diced, peeled cooked beetroot.

Cabbage Salad (*Salade de Choux*) Finely shred ½ small red or white cabbage. If using red cabbage, immediately toss with 2 tablespoons vinegar from a double quantity vinaigrette (page 91) to prevent the cabbage from discolouring. Add the remaining vinaigrette ingredients and 1 teaspoon chopped fresh dill or ½ teaspoon dill seed. Toss well. If using white cabbage, toss with vinaigrette and dill.

Carrot Salad (*Salade de Carottes*) Grate 3 large carrots, discarding the tough yellow core. Toss the grated carrots in 1 quantity vinaigrette (page 91) adding a pinch of sugar.

Fennel Salad (*Salade de Fenouil*) Trim and thinly slice 2 medium-sized fennel bulbs. Blanch for 2 minutes in lightly salted boiling water. Drain, rinse with cold water and drain thoroughly. Toss the fennel in 1 quantity vinaigrette (page 91) made with olive oil and garlic.

Pepper Salad (*Salade de Poivrons*) Core and remove the seeds from 2 red, green or yellow peppers. Slice into strips and blanch for 1 to 2 minutes in boiling water. Drain well. Toss in 1 quantity vinaigrette (page 91) made with olive oil and garlic.

Niçoise Salad

Salade Niçoise

1 (45-g/1¾-oz) can anchovy fillets, drained
4 tablespoons milk
350 g/12 oz French beans
1 (198-g/7-oz) can tuna in oil, drained and flaked
double quantity vinaigrette (page 91) made with lemon juice, olive oil and garlic
1 small or ½ large cucumber, peeled and thinly sliced
40 g/1½ oz black olives, halved and stoned
3 medium-sized tomatoes, peeled and cut in quarters

Soak the anchovy fillets in milk for 30 minutes. Drain and rinse with cold water; drain thoroughly. In a large saucepan, boil enough salted water to cover the French beans generously. Add the beans and boil for 8 to 10 minutes until just tender. Drain well. Split the anchovy fillets lengthwise with a knife. Spread the tuna on the bottom of a salad bowl. Cover with green beans. Moisten with a little vinaigrette and cover completely with cucumber, overlapping the slices to make a flat layer. Spoon most of the remaining vinaigrette over the cucumber layer. Arrange the anchovy fillets in a lattice pattern on top. Place an olive half cut-side down in the centre of each lattice. Arrange the tomato quarters around the edge of the salad and brush with the remaining vinaigrette. Niçoise Salad can be made up to 8 hours ahead, covered and refrigerated. **Serves 4**

Celeriac with Mayonnaise

Céleri-Rave Rémoulade

If you can't find celeriac, use stalk celery but do not blanch it.

1 medium-sized celeriac
juice of 1 lemon
150 ml/$\frac{1}{4}$ pint mayonnaise (page 73)
2 teaspoons French mustard
salt and pepper

Peel the celeriac and rub with lemon juice to prevent discolouration. Cut into julienne strips. If the celeriac is pleasantly crunchy, leave raw. If tough and fibrous, cover the strips with cold water, bring to the boil and blanch by boiling for 1 minute or until cooked but still crunchy. Drain.

Combine the mayonnaise with the mustard and stir in the celeriac. Season to taste with salt, pepper and mustard. Cover and leave to stand for 1 to 2 hours at room temperature to blend the flavours. Serve at room temperature. **Serves 4–6**

Beetroot Salad with Nuts

Salade de Betteraves aux Noix

An unusual combination for a refreshing winter salad.

2 heads chicory
100 g/4 oz lamb's lettuce (corn salad) or a very small lettuce
2 large beetroot, cooked
double quantity vinaigrette (page 91)
salt and pepper
50 g/2 oz walnuts, coarsely chopped

Wipe the chicory. Discard any wilted leaves and trim the stems. Cut into 2.5-cm/1-in diagonal slices. Thoroughly wash the lettuce and dry well. Mix the chicory and lettuce in a salad bowl. Just before serving, cut, peel and dice the beetroot. Add to the greens and toss the salad in the vinaigrette. Season to taste with salt and pepper. Sprinkle with walnuts before serving. **Serves 6**

Celeriac with Mayonnaise

Peel the celeriac with a sharp knife. Rub the white portion with lemon juice to prevent discolouration.

Guide the knife with your knuckles to cut thin slices before cutting it into thin strips.

Rice Salad

Salade de Riz

Be careful not to overcook the rice – it should be firm, not sticky.

225 g/8 oz long-grain rice
salt and pepper
1 slice lemon
1 carrot, diced
½ green pepper, cored, seeded and diced
½ red pepper, cored, seeded and diced
50 g/2 oz fresh or frozen peas
1 tomato, peeled, seeded and cut in strips
1 stick celery, thinly sliced
double quantity vinaigrette (page 91)

Boil plenty of salted water in a large saucepan. Add the rice and lemon and boil for 10 to 12 minutes until the rice is just tender. The lemon will keep the rice white. Drain and discard the lemon. Rinse the rice in a sieve with hot water to wash away excess starch. Poke a few drainage holes in the rice with the handle of a spoon and leave the rice in the sieve for 10 to 15 minutes to dry. Cook the carrot in boiling salted water for 5–8 minutes until tender. Drain. Rinse with cold water and drain thoroughly. Repeat this process with the peas, boiling until just tender. Not more than 2 hours before serving, carefully mix the cooked vegetables, tomato, celery and rice. Add the vinaigrette, mix well and season to taste with salt and pepper. Pile the salad in a bowl and serve at room temperature. **Serves 4**

Tomato Salad

Salade de Tomates

Home-grown ripe tomatoes are especially good in this salad.

450 g/1 lb fresh ripe tomatoes, sliced
1 teaspoon sugar
1 quantity vinaigrette (page 91) made with garlic, shallot and 1 tablespoon parsley or 1 teaspoon fresh oregano or basil
salt and pepper

Arrange the tomato slices to overlap in a serving dish. Whisk the sugar into the vinaigrette and taste for seasoning, adding extra salt and pepper, if necessary. Spoon over the tomatoes. Cover and leave to stand for 1 to 2 hours at room temperature to blend the flavours. Serve at room temperature. **Serves 4**

Vinaigrette

Vinaigrette

An excellent salad dressing to bring out the delicate flavours of a vegetable salad.

1 tablespoon vinegar or 2 teaspoons lemon juice
pinch each of salt and pepper
½ teaspoon French mustard (optional)
3 tablespoons olive or vegetable oil

Whisk the vinegar or lemon juice with the salt, pepper and mustard. Gradually whisk in the oil until the sauce is blended and slightly thickened. Taste and adjust the seasoning.

Variations

Add one or more of the following ingredients just before using: ½ clove garlic, crushed; 1 shallot, finely chopped; 1 teaspoon chopped mixed fresh herbs such as parsley, tarragon, chives, basil or oregano.

Desserts

The range of French desserts is enormous, from rich creams and mousses to delicate fresh fruit dishes.

Coming at the end of the meal as it does, a dessert must have impact. Take care with presentation – even simple Pears in Red Wine deserve a pretty dish. And where would Chocolate Mousse be without its rosette of whipped cream, or Peach Melba without its raspberry sauce? Pay attention to texture so that your soufflés are airy and your ice creams creamy and deliciously rich. Above all, emphasise flavour, adding lemon juice to develop the tartness of fruits and vanilla to enhance chocolate and coffee. Here the French often turn to liqueurs, combining rum with chocolate, Calvados with apples and Kirsch with other fruits. For a milder flavour, Cointreau and Grand Marnier blend with almost anything.

Techniques for Making Desserts

Many desserts contain eggs, so making them can amount to an exercise in egg cookery. For soufflés and mousses that rely on egg whites for lightness, it is very important to whip the whites stiffly and fold them in as lightly as possible. Many cold and frozen desserts are thickened with egg yolks which will curdle if overheated or cooked too long. So, when egg yolks are part of a custard mixture, as in Caramel Cream or Petits Pots de Crème, cooking is done in a water bath to control the temperature. For mousses and custard sauce, when the mixtures are cooked over direct heat, you must always keep the temperature low. And don't expect egg yolks to thicken a custard or a sauce in the same way as flour does – the effect will be gradual and the finished mixture light and smooth.

For the best ice creams and sorbets, constant mixing during freezing is necessary to break up ice crystals which would give the mixture a rough texture. In a traditional churn freezer, the mixture is poured into a central container surrounded by ice and salt, and beaten as it freezes with a paddle turned by a crank or by electricity. You can also get electric machines that go directly inside the freezer, saving the bother with ice and salt. Both ice cream and sorbet can be made in an ordinary freezer without churning if the mixture is thoroughly beaten several times during freezing.

Getting Ahead

Cold and frozen desserts have to be made ahead; just put them in the freezer or refrigerator and they will wait for you. However, bear in mind that although ice cream will keep up to three months without spoiling, and sorbet for up to four weeks, both taste best and are smoothest when freshly made. If a frozen dessert has been stored in the freezer for more than 12 hours, leave it in the refrigator for one or two hours before serving so that it softens enough to make spooning easy. The flavour will be better too. Remember to chill serving spoons and bowls.

Many hot desserts can be prepared ahead and reheated, notably crêpes. Unfilled, they keep well for two to three days in the refrigator or for up to a month in the freezer, and when filled they can usually wait an hour or two for the final cooking or flaming. Even for soufflés a good deal of preparation can be done in advance, though it is risky to whip up the egg whites ahead. However, once in the oven, the French dictum that 'a soufflé never waits for guests, it is they who must wait for the soufflé' is the unbreakable law.

Apple Charlotte

Charlotte aux Pommes

One of the traditional French desserts–delicious with vanilla custard sauce, *see page 99.*

175 g/6 oz butter
1.75 kg/4 lb cooking apples, cored and thinly sliced
1 vanilla pod, split lengthwise
1 thinly pared strip of lemon rind
few drops of lemon juice
pinch of cinnamon
6 oz/175 g sugar
1 teaspoon Calvados or other apple brandy (optional)
1 tablespoon apricot jam
8 to 10 slices firm white bread, crusts removed

Spread the bottom of a large heavy saucepan with 50 g/2 oz butter; add the apple slices, vanilla pod, lemon rind, lemon juice and cinnamon. Press a piece of buttered foil over the apples and cover with a lid. Cook over low heat until the apples are very soft, stirring occasionally. Remove the vanilla pod and lemon rind. Add the sugar, stirring constantly over medium heat until the purée is so thick that it barely falls from the spoon. If the purée is too soft, the charlotte will collapse when unmoulded. Add the Calvados and apricot jam. Simmer for 1 minute. Add more sugar if wished. Preheat the oven to moderately hot (200 C, 400 F, gas 6).

Place a round of buttered greaseproof paper in the bottom of a 1-litre/1½-pint charlotte mould or other straight-sided ovenproof dish. Clarify 75 g/3 oz butter (page 12). Cut 14 to 16 fingers of bread 3.5 cm/1.5 in wide to line the sides of the mould and 4 to 6 triangular pieces for the bottom of the mould. Reserve 3 or 4 bread fingers for the top of the mould. Dip, but do not soak, one side of each piece of bread in the melted butter and overlap the bread fingers butter side out in the mould. Place the bread triangles butter side down in the bottom of the mould. Fill in any holes with small pieces of bread dipped in melted butter. Spoon the apple mixture into the mould and mound the top slightly as it shrinks during baking. Cover with the reserved bread fingers and dot with the remaining butter.

Bake for 15 minutes or until the bread begins to brown. Reduce the heat to moderate (180 C, 350 F, gas 4) and bake for 40 to 50 minutes longer until the charlotte is firm and the sides are golden brown. Ease the bread slightly away from the sides of the mould to check browning. To serve hot, let the charlotte stand for 10 to 15 minutes before unmoulding on to a hot plate. To serve cold, chill the charlotte before unmoulding. **Serves 6**

Apple Crêpes

Crêpes Normande

Calvados, a type of apple brandy, is an ideal flavouring for apple desserts.

40 to 50 g/1½ to 2 oz butter
450 g/1 lb cooking apples, peeled, cored and thinly sliced
2 to 3 tablespoons caster sugar
2–3 tablespoons single cream
3 tablespoons Calvados or other apple brandy
12 to 16 crêpes (page 28)
SAUCE
150 ml/¼ pint double cream
1 tablespoon sugar
2 tablespoons Calvados or other apple brandy

Melt the butter in a frying pan. Add the apple slices and sauté for 2 to 3 minutes. Sprinkle with sugar, toss to coat and cook for 1 to 2 minutes longer until caramelised, turning occasionally. The apples should be tender but not soft. Stir in the single cream.

In a small saucepan, boil the double cream for the sauce until reduced by half. Stir in the sugar and 2 tablespoons Calvados. Boil for a further 1 minute. Grease a 1-litre/1½-pints ovenproof dish. Spoon 2 tablespoons apple mixture on each crêpe and roll into cigar shapes. Arrange in the prepared baking dish. Preheat the oven to moderately hot (200 C, 400 F, gas 6) 30 minutes before serving. Bake the crêpes for 8 to 10 minutes until very hot. Flame the crêpes with the rest of the Calvados and serve immediately. Serve the sauce separately.

Crêpes Suzette

Crêpes Suzette

A classic dessert, supposedly created to honour a lady friend of Edward VII when he was Prince of Wales.

100 g/4 oz butter
100 g/4 oz caster sugar
grated rind of 1 orange
2–3 tablespoons Grand Marnier
12 to 16 crêpes (page 28)
2 to 3 tablespoons brandy

Cream 50 g/2 oz butter with the sugar and orange rind until soft and light. Beat in 1 tablespoon of the Grand Marnier. Spread the butter mixture on the underside of each crêpe, stacking the crêpes on top of each other. Heat 1 to 2 tablespoons butter in a chafing dish or frying pan. Place a crêpe butter side down in chafing dish. Heat for 30 seconds or until very hot. Fold in half twice, underside folded to the inside, making a triangle. Leave at the side of chafing dish or frying pan. Repeat with the remaining crêpes. When all the crêpes are heated and folded, the butter and sugar should have caramelised in the bottom of the pan, adding flavour to the crêpes.

In a small saucepan heat the brandy and remaining Grand Marnier. Pour over the crêpes and carefully ignite. **Serves 4**

Raspberry Mousse

Mousse aux Framboises

If keeping Raspberry Mousse more than one day, do not use a metal mould or the mousse will discolour.

275 g/10 oz fresh raspberries
1 tablespoon water
juice of ½ lemon
15 g/½ oz powdered gelatine
3 eggs
2 egg yolks
150 g/5 oz sugar
300 ml/½ pint double cream
1 tablespoon kirsch
DECORATION
Chantilly Cream (page 117) made with 150 ml/¼ pint double cream
6 to 8 fresh whole raspberries

Reserve a few raspberries for decoration and purée the remainder in a liquidiser. Sieve to remove seeds. In a small bowl mix 1 tablespoon water with the lemon juice. Sprinkle the gelatine over the mixture and leave to stand for 5 minutes or until spongy. Beat the eggs with the egg yolks and sugar until blended, then place the bowl over a pan of hot but not boiling water and whisk until the mixture leaves a trail. Remove from the heat. Beat the softened gelatine into the hot egg mixture. Beat the mixture until cool. Rinse a 1.5-litre/2½-pint ring mould with cold water. Stir the raspberry purée into the cool egg mixture and chill until just beginning to thicken. Meanwhile lightly whip the cream. Fold the cream and kirsch into the mousse mixture. Pour into the mould. Cover and chill for at least 2 hours or until firm.

Not more than 2 hours before serving, unmould the mousse by running a knife around the edges and dipping the bottom of the mould in lukewarm water for a few seconds, then turn out on to a serving plate. Decorate the mousse with piped Chantilly Cream and the reserved raspberries. **Serves 6–8**

Raspberry Mousse (above).

Iced Praline Parfait

Parfait Praliné

Praline is a mixture of caramel and toasted almonds which can be ground and used to flavour desserts.

175 g/6 oz sugar
50 g/2 oz whole unblanched almonds
3 tablespoons water
4 egg yolks
300 ml/½ pint double cream, lightly whipped

Grease a baking sheet. Combine 50 g/2 oz of the sugar and the almonds in a small heavy saucepan. Heat over low heat, stirring occasionally, until the sugar dissolves and starts to brown. Continue stirring over low heat until the mixture is deep brown and the almonds pop, indicating they are toasted. Be careful not to allow the caramel to burn. Immediately pour the hot praline on to the prepared baking sheet. Leave to cool and when hard, break into pieces. Grind a few pieces at a time to a fine powder (the grinder attachment of a liquidiser will do this very well).

Heat the remaining sugar with 3 tablespoons water until the sugar dissolves. Bring to the boil and boil to soft ball stage (115 C/240 F on a sugar thermometer). At this temperature the syrup will form a soft ball when a little is lowered by spoon into a cup of cold water and is immediately removed from the spoon while under water. Beat the egg yolks in a bowl until slightly thickened. Let the bubbles in the hot sugar mixture subside, then pour gradually over the egg yolks, beating constantly. If using an electric mixer pour the syrup in a thin stream between the beaters and the bowl so the syrup doesn't stick to either. Increase the speed to high and continue beating until the mixture is thick and cool. Stir in the praline powder, reserving a little for decoration, then fold in the softly whipped cream. Spoon the mixture into chilled parfait glasses, sprinkle with reserved praline powder and freeze for at least 4 hours. **Serves 4**

Variations

Iced Chocolate Parfait (*Parfait au Chocolat*) Omit the praline. Melt 150 g/5 oz plain chocolate, coarsely chopped, over boiling water. Cool but do not allow to set before adding to the cool yolk mixture. Continue beating until completely cool before folding in the whipped cream. Decorate with crystallised violets or a rosette of Chantilly Cream (page 117).

Iced Coffee Parfait (*Parfait au Café*) Omit the praline. Dissolve 1 tablespoon instant coffee powder in 3 tablespoons hot water and beat into cool yolk mixture. Sprinkle the parfait with a little powdered coffee or top with a rosette of Chantilly Cream (page 117).

How to Tell if Egg Custard is Cooked

When ready, egg custard thickens only slightly. If overcooked, it will curdle because the egg yolks coagulate, in effect forming sweet scrambled eggs. Custard is close to thickening point when most of the white foam on top disappears, leaving the surface an even yellow colour. At this point remove the sauce from the heat and lift out the wooden spoon. Always use a wooden spoon for stirring – not a whisk. The custard should coat the spoon lightly. Draw a finger across the back of the spoon: it should leave a clear trail in the custard. If the trail quickly disappears, the custard is not thick enough and should be cooked for about 30 seconds longer before testing again.

Vanilla Ice Cream

Glace à la Vanille

The little black dots in this vanilla ice cream are the seeds from the vanilla pod – a sign of authenticity.

600 ml/1 pint milk
1 vanilla pod, split lengthwise
6 egg yolks
100 g/4 oz vanilla or caster sugar
300 ml/½ pint double cream, whipped lightly

Scald the milk with the vanilla pod by bringing it just to the boil. Cover, remove from the heat and leave to stand for 10 to 15 minutes. Beat the egg yolks with the sugar until light and slightly thickened. Whisk half the hot milk into the egg yolk mixture. Whisk the mixture back into the remaining milk. Stir constantly with a wooden spoon over low heat until the custard thickens slightly. Do not overcook or the custard will curdle. Immediately remove from the heat and strain into a medium bowl, removing the vanilla pod, but scraping the seeds into the custard. Cool the custard and pour into a freezer-proof container. Freeze until slushy, then whisk thoroughly. Repeat this process then fold in the cream and freeze the mixture until firm. **Makes about 1.25 litre/2 pints**

Peach Melba

Pêches Melba

This is the real Peach Melba, created by the famous chef Escoffier in honour of the singer Dame Nellie Melba.

50 g/2 oz sugar
300 ml/$\frac{1}{2}$ pint water
pared rind of 1 lemon
1 vanilla pod, split lengthwise
4 ripe peaches, halved
Chantilly Cream (page 117) made with 150 ml/$\frac{1}{4}$ pint cream
600 ml/1 pint Vanilla Ice Cream (page 96)
Melba Sauce (see below)

In a small heavy saucepan, heat the sugar with the water until the sugar dissolves. Add the lemon rind and vanilla pod. Completely immerse the peach halves cut side up in the sugar mixture. Poach them gently for 8 to 12 minutes until just tender. Remove from the heat. Leave the peaches to cool in the syrup to lukewarm. Peel the peaches and chill in the syrup. Chill 4 sundae glasses.

Not more than 2 hours before serving, prepare the Chantilly Cream and spoon it into a piping bag fitted with a medium nozzle. Just before serving, place a scoop of Vanilla Ice Cream in each of the 4 sundae glasses and arrange 2 drained peach halves on each side of the ice cream. Coat the peaches with Melba Sauce and top with a rosette of Chantilly Cream. **Serves 4**

Melba Sauce

Sauce Melba

Pour this over your favourite ice cream to create a special dessert.

225 g/8 oz raspberries
1 tablespoon kirsch
3 to 4 tablespoons icing sugar (optional)

Purée the raspberries in a blender and strain to remove any seeds. Add the kirsch and icing sugar to taste.

Strawberry Charlotte Malakoff

Charlotte Malakoff aux Fraises

Ground almonds give body and richness to this fruit charlotte.

12 to 14 sponge fingers
3 tablespoons kirsch
225 g/8 oz fresh strawberries, hulled
100 g/4 oz unsalted butter
175 g/6 oz sugar
175 g/6 oz whole blanched almonds, ground
1 tablespoon kirsch
150 ml/$\frac{1}{4}$ pint double cream, lightly whipped
Chantilly Cream (page 117) made with 150 ml/$\frac{1}{4}$ pint cream for decoration

Butter a 1.5-pint/$2\frac{1}{2}$-pint charlotte mould or soufflé dish. Line the bottom of the mould with a circle of greaseproof paper. Line the sides with sponge fingers, trimming to fit tightly. Sprinkle the remaining sponge fingers with 2 tablespoons kirsch. Slice the strawberries, reserving 6 whole ones for decoration. Cream the butter, gradually adding sugar. Continue beating until the mixture is light and fluffy. Stir in the ground almonds, kirsch and sliced strawberries. Do not beat the mixture or the almonds will become oily. Fold in the whipped cream. Spoon half the mixture into the prepared mould. Cover with the kirsch-soaked sponge fingers. Spread the remaining almond mixture evenly over the top. Cover and refrigerate for at least 4 hours or until firmly set.

Not more than 2 hours before serving, trim the tops of the sponge fingers level with the almond mixture. Unmould the charlotte on to a serving dish. Decorate the top and base with rosettes of piped Chantilly Cream and the reserved strawberries. Serve with melba sauce handed separately. **Serves 6**

Chocolate Mousse

Mousse au Chocolat

An unbeatable favourite.

175 g/6 oz plain chocolate, coarsely chopped
3 tablespoons strong black coffee
4 eggs, separated
15 g/½ oz butter
1 tablespoon rum or ½ teaspoon vanilla essence
Chantilly Cream, page 117 made with 150 ml/¼ pint cream (optional)

Melt the chocolate with the coffee in a bowl over a pan of hot water. Remove from the heat and beat in the egg yolks one by one to thicken the mixture. Beat in the butter and rum or vanilla. Allow to cool slightly. Whip the egg whites until stiff and gently fold them into the chocolate mixture. Pour into 4 ramekins or sundae glasses. Cover and chill for at least 6 hours for the flavours to blend. If liked, decorate with piped Chantilly Cream before serving. **Serves 4**

Cold Lemon Soufflé

Soufflé Froid au Citron

This cold soufflé is set in a paper collar. When the collar is removed, the mixture looks as if it has risen.

25 g/1 oz powdered gelatine
6 eggs, separated
12 oz/350 g su[illegible]
juice and grated r[illegible] 4 lemons
300 ml/½ pint double cream, lightly whipped
DECORATION
Chantilly Cream (page 117)
3 tablesp[illegible]achios, blanched and chopped [illegible]ptional)

Wrap a strip of greaseproof paper or a double thickness of foil around a 2-litre/3½-pint soufflé dish so it extends 2 to 3 inches above the edge of the dish. Fasten with sticky tape or string. Sprinkle the gelatine over 6 tablespoons cold water in a small pan and leave for 5 minutes until spongy. In a large bowl, beat the egg yolks, two-thirds of the sugar, lemon juice and peel until blended. Place the bowl o[illegible]an of hot but not boiling water. Whisk until the mixture is light and thick enough to leave a trail. Remove from the heat. Melt the softened gelatine over very low heat and beat into the lemon mixture. Continue beating until the mixture is cool. Whip the egg whites until stiff. Add the remaining sugar and beat for a further 20 seconds to make a light meringue. Chill the lemon mixture, stirring frequently until it starts to thicken. Fold in the cream, followed by the meringue. Fill the prepared souffl[illegible] Chill for at least 2 hours.

Not more than 2 hours before serving, prepare the Chantilly Cream. Trim the paper collar level with the soufflé mixture. Spread the top of the soufflé with Chantilly Cream and mark a diamond pattern with a knife point. Pipe the remainder in rosettes around the edge of the soufflé. Remove the paper collar just before serving and press the pistachios around the sides of the soufflé. **Serves 8**

Chocolate Mousse: folding the egg whites into the chocolate mixture.

Petits Pots de Crème

Petits Pots de Crème

A speciality of Maxim's Restaurant in Paris. They come in three flavours so each guest can choose two or three.

75 g/3 oz plain chocolate, coarsely chopped
[illegible] ml/$1\frac{1}{2}$ pints milk
1 [illegible] pod, split lengthwise
[illegible] egg yolks
[illegible]g/6 oz sugar
2 teaspoons instant coffee powder
1 teaspoon hot water

Preheat the oven to moderate ([illegible]°C, [illegible]°F, gas 3). Melt the chocolate in a bowl over a pan of boiling water. Allow to cool slightly. Scald the milk with the vanilla pod by bringing it just to the boil. Cover, remove from the heat and leave to stand for 10 to 15 minutes. Remove the vanilla pod. Beat the egg yolks with the sugar until pale and slightly thickened. Whisk in the hot milk, then strain the mixture into a jug. Pour a third of the mixture equally into four custard pots or ramekins. Dissolve the coffee powder in 1 teaspoon hot water and stir into the remaining custard. Pour half this custard equally into 4 more custard pots. Stir the melted chocolate into the remaining custard and fill the last 4 custard pots. Although the last custard mixture combines vanilla, coffee and chocolate, chocolate will predominate. Skim off any surface bubbles with a spoon.

Cover the custard pots with lids or foil and place in a water bath (page 16). Bring just to the boil, then transfer to the oven. Bake for 25 to 30 minutes until almost set and a knife inserted in the centre comes out clean. Reduce the oven temperature if the water starts to boil or the custard may curdle. Remove the pots from the water bath. Serve cold. **Serves 4–6**

Custard Sauce

Crème Anglaise

This sauce is delicious served hot or cold with fresh or poached fruit.

300 ml/$\frac{1}{2}$ pint milk
1 vanilla pod, split lengthwise *or* 1 to 2 teaspoons grated lemon or orange rind
4 egg yolks
2 tablespoons caster sugar

Scald the milk with the vanilla pod by bringing it just to the boil. If using grated lemon or orange rind, scald the milk without flavouring. Remove from the heat, cover and leave to stand for 10 to 15 minutes. Beat the egg yolks with the sugar until thick and pale. Strain in half the hot milk, then whisk back into the remaining hot milk. Using a wooden spoon, stir constantly in a pan or double boiler over medium heat until the custard thickens enough to leave a trail on the spoon. Do not boil or the custard will curdle. Immediately remove from the heat and strain into a bowl. Add the grated lemon or orange rind, if using. Cool completely, then chill in the refrigerator. **Makes 300 ml/$\frac{1}{2}$ pint**

Placing Pots de Crème in a water bath.

Caramel Cream

Crème Caramel

Individual moulds are lined with caramel which becomes a sauce when cooked and unmoulded.

CARAMEL
100 g/4 oz granulated sugar
3 tablespoons water
CUSTARD
450 ml/$\frac{3}{4}$ pint milk
1 vanilla pod, split lengthwise
50 g/2 oz sugar
2 eggs
2 egg yolks

In a small heavy saucepan, gently heat the sugar and water until the sugar is completely dissolved. Boil until caramelised. Remove from the heat and let the bubbles subside.

Pour the hot caramel into a 900-ml/1$\frac{1}{2}$-pint soufflé dish, cream caramel moulds or small ramekins. Immediately turn the dish or dishes to coat the base and sides evenly with caramel. Allow to cool completely. Preheat the oven to moderate (180 C, 350 F, gas 4). Scald the milk with the vanilla pod by bringing it just to the boil. Remove from the heat. Cover, and leave to stand for 10 to 15 minutes. Remove the vanilla pod. Add the sugar and stir until dissolved.

Beat the eggs with the egg yolks until well mixed, then stir in the hot milk. Cool slightly and strain into the prepared dish or dishes. Place in a water bath. Transfer to the oven and bake for 40 to 50 minutes if the custard is in one large dish or 20 to 25 minutes if in individual dishes. Reduce the oven temperature if the water starts to boil or the custard may curdle. The custard is done when it is set and a knife inserted in the centre comes out clean. Remove the dish or dishes from the water bath and leave to cool. Not more than 1 hour before serving, run a knife round the edge of the custard and turn out onto a deep platter or serving plates. **Serves 4–6**

Caramel Bavarian Cream

Bavarois au Caramel

Bavarian cream is a custard dessert, lightly set with gelatine.

15 g/$\frac{1}{2}$ oz powdered gelatine
6 egg yolks
6 tablespoons sugar
350 ml/12 fl oz milk
150 ml/$\frac{1}{4}$ pint cream, lightly whipped
150 ml/$\frac{1}{4}$ pint water
Chantilly Cream (page 117) to decorate
CARAMEL SYRUP
225 g/8 oz sugar
4 tablespoons cold water
150 ml/$\frac{1}{4}$ pint hot water

Prepare the caramel syrup. In a small heavy saucepan, gently heat the sugar with the cold water until the sugar dissolves. Boil until the syrup caramelises. Remove from the heat immediately, cover the hand holding the pan with a tea-towel and add the hot water. Stand back as the caramel will spatter. Heat over low heat until the caramel dissolves.

In a small bowl, sprinkle the gelatine over 2 tablespoons cold water. Leave to stand for 5 minutes or until spongy. Rinse a 900-ml/1$\frac{1}{2}$-pint mould with cold water. Beat the egg yolks and sugar until pale and creamy. Scald the milk by bringing it just to the boil. Whisk half the hot milk into the egg yolk mixture, then whisk the mixture back into the remaining hot milk. Stir constantly with a wooden spoon over low heat until the custard thickens slightly. Do not overcook the custard or it will curdle. Remove from the heat and strain into a bowl. Add the softened gelatine and stir until completely dissolved. Add half the caramel syrup and cool, stirring occasionally. Chill the custard, stirring frequently until it starts to thicken. Fold in the cream and pour the mixture into the prepared mould. Cover and refrigerate for at least 2 hours or until firm.

Heat the remaining caramel syrup with the remaining 150 ml/$\frac{1}{4}$ pint water and leave to cool for the sauce. Not more than 2 hours before serving, unmould the cream by carefully running a knife around the edges and dipping the bottom of the mould in lukewarm water for a few seconds. Turn out on to a serving plate. Decorate with piped Chantilly Cream and serve with the caramel sauce handed separately. **Serves 6–8**

Chocolate Soufflé

Soufflé au Chocolat

Baked as directed, the top of the soufflé will be crusty and the centre will be creamy.

125 g/4½ oz plain chocolate, coarsely chopped
6 tablespoons double cream
3 egg yolks
few drops vanilla essence
1½ teaspoons brandy
5 egg whites
3 tablespoons caster sugar
1 tablespoon icing sugar

Thickly butter a 1-litre/1½-pint soufflé dish, being sure the edge is buttered well so the mixture won't stick. Sprinkle the buttered dish with a little of the sugar, tapping the sides to distribute evenly; pour out excess. Melt the chocolate in the cream in a bowl over a pan of hot water. Remove from the heat and beat the egg yolks into the hot mixture to thicken it. Stir in the vanilla essence and brandy. Chocolate Soufflé can be prepared to this point 3 to 4 hours ahead.

Preheat the oven to hot (220 C, 425 F, gas 7). Whip the egg whites until stiff. Add the sugar and beat for a further 20 seconds to make a light meringue. Heat the chocolate mixture until hot to the touch. Remove from the heat and stir in a little of the meringue. Add the chocolate mixture to the remaining meringue and fold together as lightly as possible. Spoon into the prepared mould. Bake for 12 to 15 minutes until risen and a crust has formed on top. Sprinkle with icing sugar and serve immediately. **Serves 4**

Grand Marnier Soufflé

Soufflé Grand Marnier

250 ml/8 fl oz milk
3 egg yolks
grated rind of 2 oranges
50 g/2 oz sugar
2 tablespoons plain flour
2 to 3 tablespoons Grand Marnier
5 egg whites
1 tablespoon icing sugar

Thickly butter a 1.5-litre/2-pint soufflé dish, being sure the edge is buttered well so the mixture won't stick. Sprinkle the buttered dish with a little of the sugar, tapping the sides to distribute evenly; pour out the excess. In a medium saucepan, scald the milk by bringing it just to the boil. Beat the egg yolks with the orange rind and 25 g/1 oz of the sugar until thick and pale. Stir in the flour. Whisk in half the hot milk, then whisk back into the remaining hot milk. Bring to the boil, whisking constantly until the mixture thickens. Cook over low heat for 2 minutes, whisking constantly until the mixture thins slightly, indicating that the flour is cooked. Cool to lukewarm and stir in the Grand Marnier. Grand Marnier Soufflé can be prepared to this point 3 to 4 hours ahead, covered and refrigerated.

Preheat the oven to hot (220 C, 425 F, gas 7). Whip the egg whites until stiff. Add the remaining 2 tablespoons sugar and beat for a further 20 seconds to make a light meringue. Heat the Grand Marnier mixture until hot to the touch, then remove from the heat and stir in a little of the meringue. Add to the remaining meringue and fold together as lightly as possible. Spoon into the prepared dish. Bake for 12 to 15 minutes until risen and browned. Sprinkle with icing sugar and serve immediately. **Serves 4**

Pears in Red Wine

Poires au Vin Rouge

Poaching pears in red wine gives them a pretty pink colour.

100 g/4 oz sugar
400 ml/1½ pints red wine
1 strip of lemon rind
1 (5-cm/2-in) piece cinnamon stick
6 firm pears
lemon juice or caster sugar to taste

Choose a saucepan that just fits the pears standing upright. In the saucepan, gently heat the sugar, wine, lemon rind and cinnamon stick until the sugar has dissolved. Boil the syrup for 5 minutes and cool slightly. Peel the pears and then carefully remove the core from the base, leaving the stem on top. Cut a thin slice off the bottom so the pears stand upright. Immerse the pears in the syrup, adding more wine to cover, if necessary. Cover the saucepan and simmer gently for 20 to 45 minutes until tender. The cooking time will depend on the variety and ripeness of the pears, but 20 minutes is the minimum to prevent discolouration around the cores.

Allow the pears to cool, then drain, reserving the syrup. Arrange the pears in a shallow dish. Strain the syrup into a saucepan and gently simmer until thick enough to coat the back of a spoon; do not let the syrup caramelise. Taste, adding lemon juice or sugar if desired. Cool slightly and spoon over the pears. Serve chilled with Chantilly Cream (page 117). **Serves 6**

Pears Belle Hélène

Poires Belle Hélène

Homemade ice cream can be replaced by shop-bought ice cream, but do make the chcolate suace!

100 g/4 oz sugar
450 ml/¾ pint water
pared rind of 1 lemon
1 vanilla pod, split lengthwise
4 ripe pears
juice of 1 lemon
600 ml/1 pint Vanilla Ice Cream (page 96)
CHOCOLATE SAUCE
100 g/4 oz plain chocolate, chopped
4 tablespoons double cream
25 g/1 oz butter, cut in pieces
½ teaspoon vanilla essence or 1 tablespoon rum

Choose a saucepan that just fits the pears standing upright. Heat the sugar and water in saucepan until the sugar is dissolved. Add the lemon rind and vanilla pod. Simmer for 5 minutes. Peel the pears, leaving the stems on, and rub with lemon juice to prevent discolouration. Carefully remove the core from the bottom of each pear. Cut a thin slice from the bottom of each pear so they stand upright. Immerse the pears in the syrup, adding more water to cover, if necessary. Gently simmer the pears in sugar syrup for 20 to 25 minutes until tender. Remove from the heat.

Allow the pears to cool in the sugar syrup, then drain and chill. While the pears are cooling prepare the chocolate sauce. Melt the chocolate with the cream in a bowl over a pan of hot water, stirring often. When the mixture is smooth, remove from the heat and add the butter, piece by piece. Stir in the vanilla essence or rum.

Just before serving, reheat the chocolate sauce. Flatten a scoop of Vanilla Ice Cream in each of four dessert dishes and place a pear on top. Covei with hot chocolate sauce and serve immediately. **Serves 4**

Pears Belle Hélène (above).

Cakes and Pastries

French pastry chefs often say their whole repertoire is built on only a few basic recipes. Master some of these – choux and puff pastry, Génoise and crème au beurre, for instance – and a vast range of delicious cakes and pastries will be open to you.

Basic Rules for Cakes and Pastries

In cake and pastry making, more than in any other branch of cooking, it is attention to detail that counts. Be sure you understand the proper consistency for the mixture you are making.

When making pastry, lightness of touch and the temperature at which you work are important. Speed is essential; the longer a dough is worked the more elastic it becomes, so it is hard to roll, and becomes tough.

Many French pastries, particularly puff pastry, contain a high proportion of butter and special precautions must be taken to prevent the butter from melting. Chill the work surface by setting a tray of ice on it, and chill the rolling pin and flour in the freezer, then work fast. Once in the oven, the richer the dough, the higher the cooking temperature should be. When the pastry starts to brown, the heat may be reduced.

Getting Ahead

Puff pastry takes most kindly to storage. It freezes well, baked or unbaked. It can be kept 24 hours in the refrigerator before baking, or two to three days in an airtight container when cooked.

Shortcrust pastry can be baked a day or two ahead and kept tightly sealed. Unbaked dough dries out in the freezer and will lose lightness if it is refrigerated for more than a few days.

Choux pastry is even less accommodating. Uncooked dough must be kept tightly sealed and used within 8 hours. It cannot be frozen. Cooked choux puffs become tough after a day or so.

Cakes are another matter. Those containing butter and nuts will keep well for a few days in an airtight container and most cakes freeze excellently, including those iced with crème au beurre.

How to Prepare Cake Tins and Baking Sheets

Cake tins and baking sheets are usually greased except for mixtures with a high fat content such as puff pastry.

Flour used as coating on a baking sheet helps give cakes a smooth surface and discourages mixtures from spreading.

Water sprinkled on a baking sheet holds puff pastry in shape and prevents shrinkage. The steam generated also helps dough rise.

Sponge Cakes Grease the cake tin by brushing it with very soft or melted butter. Cut a circle of greaseproof paper the same diameter as the base of the tin and grease it too. Sprinkle the tin with flour, turn it upside down and tap it sharply to dislodge excess flour. For a crisp crust, sprinkle the pan with sugar before sprinkling with flour. Be careful not to finger the surface.

Meringues and Sponge Fingers Brush a baking sheet generously with butter, especially for meringues which tend to stick. Sprinkle it with flour and tap to dislodge excess.

Yeast Doughs Butter the tin or baking sheet.

Choux Pastry Butter the baking sheet lightly.

Puff Pastry Sprinkle a little water on the baking sheet.

Shortcrust Pastry Plain flan tins need only be lightly buttered. However, fluted tins should be well buttered.

How to Check Whether Cakes Are Done

When you start to *smell* a cake baking, begin checking it. When you see that the cake has shrunk slightly from the edges of the pan, it is probably cooked. If you press the centre gently with your finger, the cake should feel firm and the finger mark should disappear. Or, insert a thin skewer in the cake – if there is no mixture sticking to it when it is withdrawn, the cake is done.

Walnut Cake

Biscuit aux Noix

100 to 175 g/4 to 6 oz walnut halves
50 g/2 oz butter
40 g/1½ oz flour
3 egg yolks
150 g/5 oz caster sugar
few drops vanilla essence
1 to 2 tablespoons kirsch (optional)
4 egg whites
100 g/4 oz granulated sugar
FILLING
Coffee Crème au Beurre (page 106) made with 4 egg yolks
100 g/4 oz walnut halves, coarsely chopped

Line the bottom and grease the sides of an 18-cm/7-in springform cake tin. Preheat the oven to moderate (180 C, 350 F, gas 4). Reserve 10 to 15 walnut halves for decoration and grind the remainder in the grinder attachment of a liquidiser or in a food processor. In a bowl over a pan of hot water melt the butter until very soft but not oily.

Sift the flour and mix with the ground walnuts. In a large bowl, beat the egg yolks with 100 g/4 oz of the caster sugar until the mixture is light and thick enough to leave a trail. Beat in the vanilla essence and 1 tablespoon kirsch, if desired. Whip the egg whites until stiff and add the remaining sugar and beat for 30 seconds to make a light meringue. Gently fold the flour and walnut mixture and meringue into the yolk mixture, alternating a third of the flour mixture with half the meringue. Fold in the butter with the last addition of flour. The mixture quickly loses volume after the butter is added, so fold it in as quickly and gently as possible. Pour the mixture into the prepared tin. Bake for 40 to 50 minutes until the cake shrinks slightly from the sides of the pan and the cake top springs back when touched. Run a knife around the sides of the cake, and turn onto a rack to cool.

Put the granulated sugar in a small saucepan with 6 tablespoons water. Heat gently until dissolved then stir in the remaining kirsch.

Cut the thoroughly cooled cake in 2 or 3 layers with a long serrated knife. Gently brush the cut side of each layer with sugar syrup. Spread the layers thinly with crème au beurre and sprinkle each layer with chopped walnuts, reserving a little crème au beurre for decoration; spread the top and sides of the cake with crème au beurre from a piping bag fitted with a medium star nozzle. Top each rosette with a walnut half. **Serves 6–8**

Coffee Roll

Biscuit Roulé au Café

Sprinkling rum over the cake not only adds flavour but helps keep the cake moist.

65 g/2½ oz flour
pinch of salt
4 eggs, separated
150 g/5 oz caster sugar
few drops vanilla essence
Coffee Crème au Beurre (page 106) made with 3 egg yolks
1–2 tablespoons rum (optional)

Preheat the oven to moderately hot (190 C, 375 F, gas 5). Line and grease a 28 × 33-cm/11 × 13-in Swiss roll tin. Sift the flour with the salt. In a large bowl, beat the egg yolks with two-thirds of the sugar until light and thick enough to leave a trail. Beat in the vanilla. In another bowl whip the egg whites until stiff, add the remaining sugar and beat for a further 30 seconds to make a light meringue. Gently fold the flour and meringue into the egg yolk mixture, alternating a third of the flour with half the meringue. Pour the mixture into the prepared Swiss roll tin and spread out evenly. Bake for 8–10 minutes until the edges are browned.

Turn the sponge out on to a clean tea-towel, roll up with the towel and leave to cool. Unroll the cooled cake and sprinkle with the rum. Trim the edges of the cake with a sharp knife and spread the cake with half the crème au beurre. Roll up the cake, removing the tea-towel as you roll. Spread more crème au beurre over the top of the cake and trim the ends. Decorate the roll with rosettes of crème au beurre piped from a piping bag fitted with a medium star nozzle. Refrigerate until ready to serve. **Serves 6–8**

Strawberry Cake

Gâteau Fraisier

This cake uses the famous Genoese sponge as its base.

SPONGE
65 g/2½ oz plain flour
pinch of salt
40 g/1½ oz clarified butter
3 eggs
100 g/4 oz caster sugar
few drops vanilla essence
TO FINISH
100 g/4 oz sugar
2 tablespoons kirsch
Crème au Beurre (page 106) made with 3 egg yolks
450 g/1 lb strawberries, hulled
3 tablespoons redcurrant jelly, melted

Prepare a 20 to 23-cm/8 to 9-in round cake tin. Preheat the oven to moderate (180 C, 350 F, gas 4). Sift the flour with the salt twice. Clarify the butter (page 12). Place the eggs in a large bowl and gradually beat in the sugar. Beat for 8 to 10 minutes until the mixture is light and thick enough to leave a trail. Mix in the vanilla.

Sift the flour over the batter in 3 batches, gently folding in after each addition. Fold in the clarified butter with the last addition of flour. The mixture quickly loses volume after the butter is added, so fold it in as quickly and gently as possible. Pour into the prepared tin and bake for 25 to 30 minutes until the cake shrinks slightly from the sides of the pan and the top springs back when touched. Run a knife around the sides of the cake and turn out of the pan on to a rack to cool.

Put the sugar in a saucepan with 6 tablespoons water. Heat gently until dissolved then boil for 1–2 minutes. Allow to cool, and stir in 1 tablespoon kirsch. Prepare the crème au beurre and beat in the remaining 1 tablespoon kirsch. Chill in the refrigerator. Cut the thoroughly cooled sponge into two equal layers with a long serrated knife. Gently brush the cut side of each layer with the sugar syrup. Spread a thick layer of crème au beurre over the bottom half of the cake. Cover the whole strawberries, pressing them into the crème au beurre. Spread a little more crème au beurre over the strawberries. Cut the remaining strawberries in half lengthwise and press strawberry halves into the crème au beurre around the edge of the cake so they stand up straight with cut side facing out. Place the remaining layer of cake on top and spread with a thin layer of crème au beurre. Decorate with the remaining strawberry halves and glaze with the redcurrant jelly. Spoon the remaining crème au beurre into a piping bag fitted with a medium star nozzle and pipe rosettes on top. **Serves 6–8**

Butter Cream

Crème au Beurre

Add Butter Cream to a standard sponge cake and you will have a luscious gâteau.

3	**egg yolks**	4
100 g/4 oz	**sugar**	150 g/5 oz
3 tablespoons	**water**	4 tablespoons
175 g/6 oz	**unsalted butter**	225 g/8 oz

Beat the egg yolks until just mixed. In a small heavy saucepan, heat the sugar with the water until dissolved, then bring to the boil and continue to boil until the syrup reaches soft-ball stage or 115 C/240 F on a sugar thermometer. Wait until the bubbles subside, then gradually pour the hot sugar syrup over the egg yolks, beating constantly. If using an electric mixer, pour the sugar syrup in a thin stream between the beaters and the bowl so the syrup doesn't stick to either. Then beat as fast as possible until the mixture is thick and cool. Soften the butter and gradually beat it into the yolk mixture which must be quite cool or it will melt the butter when you beat it in.

Variations

Chocolate Butter Cream (*Crème au Beurre au Chocolat*) For a 3-egg yolk quantity add 100 g/4 oz plain chocolate which has been melted over a pan of boiling water. Cool slightly before beating into the crème au beurre.

Coffee Butter Cream (*Crème au Beurre au Café*) For a 3-egg yolk quantity add 3–4 teaspoons instant coffee powder dissolved in 1 tablespoon hot water.

Strawberry Cake (above).

Metz Chocolate Cake

Gâteau au Chocolat de Metz

Cornflour and ground almonds are used instead of flour, to give a rich smooth texture.

225 g/8 oz plain chocolate, broken into pieces
4 tablespoons milk
few drops vanilla essence
100 g/4 oz caster sugar
100 g/4 oz cornflour
65 g/2½ oz ground almonds
6 eggs, separated

ICING

75 g/3 oz plain chocolate, coarsely chopped
75 g/3 oz icing sugar, sifted
1 egg white
1 tablespoon warm water

Grease and line a 25 to 28-cm/10 to 11-in springform or other deep round cake tin. Preheat the oven to moderate (180 C, 350 F, gas 4). In a small heavy saucepan, melt the chocolate in the milk over low heat, stirring constantly. When the mixture is smooth, remove from the heat and beat in the vanilla, half the caster sugar and the cornflour. In a small bowl, mix the ground almonds with the egg yolks and stir into the chocolate mixture.

In a large bowl, whip the egg whites until stiff. Add the remaining caster sugar. Beat for a further 30 seconds to make a light meringue. Stir a little of the egg whites into the chocolate mixture. Gently fold the chocolate mixture into the remaining egg whites and pour into the prepared tin. Bake for 45 minutes; the cake should still be slightly soft in the centre. Cool and turn the cooled cake out of the tin on to a rack placed over a tray.

Not more than a few hours before serving, prepare the icing. Melt the chocolate over boiling water and cool slightly. Beat the icing sugar and egg white with a wooden spoon until smooth. Beat the mixture into the chocolate, then beat in the water. Pour the warm icing over the cake and spread quickly with a palette knife before the icing sets. **Serves 8–10**

Sponge Fingers

Biscuits à la Cuiller

Sponge fingers should be firm outside, soft inside and only lightly browned.

100 g/4 oz flour
pinch of salt
4 eggs, separated
100 g/4 oz sugar
½ teaspoon vanilla essence
icing sugar for sprinkling

Grease and flour a baking sheet. Preheat the oven to moderate (180 C, 350 F, gas 4). Sift the flour with the salt. In a large bowl, beat the egg yolks with half the sugar and the vanilla essence until pale and thick enough to leave a trail. In another bowl whip the egg whites until stiff, add the remaining sugar and beat for a further 30 seconds to make a light meringue. Sift the flour over the egg yolk mixture and add about a quarter of the egg whites. Fold together lightly, then fold in the rest of the whites in two batches. Gently spoon the mixture into a piping bag fitted with a plain 1-cm/½-in nozzle. Pipe biscuits on the baking sheet 8-cm/3½-in long and at least 2.5 cm/1 in apart. Sprinkle with icing sugar. Bake for 15 to 18 minutes, wedging the oven door ajar with a spoon so that the sponge fingers dry as they bake. Remove from the oven and allow to cool slightly on a baking sheet. Transfer to a rack to cool completely. **Makes 30**

Chocolate Truffles

Truffes au Chocolat

(Illustrated on front endpaper)

275 g/10 oz plain chocolate, chopped
50 g/2 oz butter
2 tablespoons strong black coffee
100 g/4 oz icing sugar, sifted
1 teaspoon brandy or rum
1 tablespoon double cream
50 g/2 oz cocoa powder

Melt 175 g/6 oz of the chocolate with the butter over a pan of hot water. Stir in the coffee, icing sugar, brandy or rum and cream. Chill for 30 to 40 minutes until fairly firm.

Spoon heaped teaspoons of the chocolate mixture on to a sheet of greaseproof paper. Shape into balls and chill for 2 hours or until firm. Melt the remaining chocolate in a bowl over a pan of hot water and put the cocoa powder in a small tray with raised edges. Spear each truffle with a wooden cocktail stick and dip in melted chocolate to coat. Quickly transfer to the cocoa powder. Spoon the powder over each truffle to cover. Leave the truffles to harden for about 1 hour at room temperature. Place on a clean sheet of greaseproof paper and remove the cocktail sticks.

Refrigerate the truffles in an airtight container with greaseproof paper between the layers. Because the flavour improves with age store the truffles for at least one week, but not longer than one month. **Makes 25**

Meringues with Whipped Cream

Meringues Chantilly

Instead of using a piping bag, you can shape the meringue into ovals with 2 tablespoons.

4 egg whites
225 g/8 oz caster sugar
few drops vanilla essence
25 g/1 oz icing sugar
Chantilly Cream (page 117) made with cream

Line two baking sheets with non-stick cooking parchment or thoroughly grease and flour the baking sheets. In a large bowl, whip the egg whites until stiff. Add 2 tablespoons of the sugar and beat for 30 seconds to make a light meringue. Fold in the remaining sugar with the vanilla essence. Gently spoon the meringue into a piping bag fitted with a 1-cm/½-in plain nozzle and pipe mounds of meringue about 7.5 cm/3 in diameter on to the prepared baking sheets. Space the mounds at least 2.5 cm/1 in apart. Generously sprinkle the meringues with icing sugar. Bake in a cool oven (140 C, 275 F, gas 1) for 1 hour or until firm. If the meringues start to brown reduce the heat to very cool (120 C, 250 F, gas ½). Remove the meringues from the baking sheet by pulling the paper off or lifting the meringues carefully with a spatula. Gently press the bottoms of the meringue to form a hollow. Return the meringues, hollow-side up, to the baking sheets. Bake for a further 30 minutes or until the shells are crisp. Meringues should be a pale cream colour with a slightly sticky centre.

Not more than 2 hours before serving, prepare the Chantilly Cream and spoon it into the hollowed meringue bottoms. Place another meringue over the Chantilly Cream to make a sandwich. **Makes 6 filled meringues**

Variations

Almond Meringues (*Rochers de Neige*) Fold ½ cup sliced almonds into the meringue mixture and spoon the mixture into rough 4-cm/1½-in mounds on the prepared baking sheet. Sprinkle with a few more sliced almonds. Bake for 1 hour or until firm on the outside but soft in the centre. Omit the Chantilly Cream. **Makes about 30**

Rich Shortcrust Pastry

Pâte Brisée

One of the secrets of pastry making is to work quickly so the mixture does not become too warm and sticky.

Ingredients to make:		
1 (23 to 25-cm/9 to 10-in) flan case or 6 (8.5-cm/$3\frac{1}{2}$-in) tartlet shells		1 (28 to 30-cm/11 to 12-in) flan case or 8 (8.5-cm/$3\frac{1}{2}$-in) tartlet shells
200 g/7 oz	**plain flour**	250 g/9 oz
100 g/$3\frac{1}{2}$ oz	**butter**	125 g/$4\frac{1}{2}$ oz
1	**egg yolk(s)**	2
$\frac{1}{2}$ teaspoon	**salt**	$\frac{3}{4}$ teaspoon
2–3 tablespoons	**cold water**	3–4 tablespoons

Sift the flour on to a flat work surface and make a well in the centre. Pound the butter with a rolling pin to soften. Place the butter, egg yolks and salt with a little of the water in the well and quickly work with the flour until partly mixed. Using the fingertips of both hands, gradually work in the flour to form coarse crumbs. If the crumbs are very dry add more water, a few drops at a time. Press the dough into a ball; it should be soft but not sticky. Flour the working surface and knead the dough lightly until smooth and pliable. Press into a ball. Wrap in greaseproof paper or cling film and chill for 30 minutes before using.

Rich Shortcrust Pastry

Far left Combine egg yolks, salt, water and softened butter. Mix lightly with your fingertips.

Centre Gradually work the flour into the butter and egg mixture with your fingertips until coarse crumbs are formed.

Left Smear the butter mixture into the flour by pushing the dough with the heel of your hand. Scrape dough from the work surface with a spatula.

Alsatian Fruit Quiche

Quiche Alsacienne aux Fruits

Preheating the baking sheet prevents the pastry from becoming soggy.

rich shortcrust pastry (page 110) made with 250 g/9 oz flour
40 g/1½ oz butter
1 kg/2 lb cooking apples, peeled, cored and thickly sliced
1 tablespoon sugar
2 eggs
1 egg yolk
100 g/4 oz caster sugar
150 ml/¼ pint single cream
few drops vanilla essence or 1 teaspoon kirsch
APRICOT JAM GLAZE
1 (350-g/12-oz) jar apricot jam
juice of ½ lemon
2 to 3 tablespoons water

Preheat the oven to moderately hot (200 C, 400 F, gas 6) and heat a baking sheet in it. Melt the butter in a frying pan, add the apples and sprinkle with 1 tablespoon sugar. Cook quickly over medium heat, shaking the pan occasionally, until the apples are lightly caramelised and almost tender. Beat the eggs, egg yolk and the sugar until thoroughly mixed. Stir in the cream and vanilla or kirsch.

Roll out the pastry (5 mm/¼ in thick) and line a 28 to 30-cm/11 to 12-in flan tin. Trim the edges and prick the base of the flan a few times. Arrange the fruit in the flan and pour the egg mixture over the apples, to fill the shell. Place the quiche on a hot baking sheet on the bottom shelf of the oven. Bake for 30 to 40 minutes until the egg mixture is set. Transfer to a rack to cool. Prepare the apricot jam glaze (below) and use 4 tablespoons to brush the cooled quiche. **Serves 6–8**

Apricot Jam Glaze

In a small non-aluminium saucepan, melt the jam with the lemon juice and enough water to make a pourable glaze. Work through a strainer and store in an airtight container. Reheat the glaze to melt before using.

Variations

Instead of the apples, use any of the following: 1 kg/2 lb pears, peeled, cored and quartered; 450 g/1 lb fresh or frozen cherries, stoned; 675 g/1½ lb plums, halved and stoned; or 675 g/1½ lb apricots, halved and stoned. Omit the step of caramelising the fruit. Arrange the fruit in the pastry shell, placing the plums and apricots cut side up so the juice does not soak the pastry.

Sweet Flan Pastry

Pâte Sucrée

Chilling this delicate dough makes it much easier to roll out.

200 g/7 oz plain flour
generous pinch salt
100 g/3½ oz sugar
4 egg yolks
few drops vanilla essence
100 g/3½ oz butter

Sift the flour on to a flat surface and make a large well in the centre. Place the salt, sugar, egg yolks and vanilla in the well and mix these ingredients with your fingertips until the sugar dissolves. Pound the butter with a rolling pin to soften. Add the butter to the well and quickly work with your fingertips until partly mixed. Gradually work in the flour to make coarse crumbs, gathering the flour up with a spatula. When the dough comes together in a ball, lightly flour the work surface and knead the dough very lightly. The dough should be smooth and pliable. Press into a ball, wrap in greaseproof paper or cling film and chill for 30 minutes. **Makes enough for 1 (28 to 30-cm/11 to 12-in) flan or 8 tartlet shells**

Lemon Pie

Tarte au Citron

(Illustrated on back endpaper)
A speciality from Provence, which is the *almond and citrus area.*

sweet flan pastry (page 112)
2 eggs
100 g/4 oz sugar
grated rind and juice of 1½ lemons
100 g/4 oz unsalted butter, clarified
100 g/4 oz ground almonds

Chill the pastry for at least 30 minutes. Preheat the oven to moderately hot (190 C, 375 F, gas 5). Roll out the pastry 5 mm/¼ in thick and use to line a 25 to 30-cm/11 to 12-in flan tin. Chill, then bake blind for 15 minutes or until the pastry is set and lightly browned. Cool slightly. Reduce the oven temperature to moderate (180 C, 350 F, gas 4).

In a large bowl, beat the eggs and sugar until pale and thick enough to leave a trail. Stir in the lemon rind and juice, followed by the melted butter and ground almonds. Pour the lemon mixture into the flan case. Bake for 20 to 25 minutes until the filling is golden brown and set. Cool. Serve the pie at room temperature within 6 to 8 hours. **Serves 6–8**

Sand Cookies

Sablés de Caen

These butter shortbread biscuits come from Normandy.

sweet flan pastry (page 112)
grated rind of 1 orange
beaten egg to glaze

Prepare the sweet flan pastry, adding the orange rind with the egg yolks. Chill for at least 30 minutes. Grease two baking sheets. Preheat the oven to moderately hot (190 C, 375 F, gas 5). Roll out the dough to 5 mm/¼ in thick. Stamp out rounds with a 8.5-cm/3½-in biscuit cutter. Place the rounds on the prepared baking sheets. Brush the biscuits with beaten egg. Using a table fork, score each biscuit with a triangular design. Chill for 10 to 15 minutes. Bake for 7 to 10 minutes until lightly browned. Do not overcook or the biscuits will be bitter. Transfer to a rack to cool. **Makes 10–12**

Almond Fruit Torte

Galette d'Amandes aux Fruits

Slanted wedges of almond pastry form a pinwheel on top of this torte.

350 g/12 oz ground almonds
125 g/4½ oz sugar
125 g/4½ oz salt
½ teaspoon salt
150 g/5 oz butter
1 egg yolk
Chantilly Cream (page 117) made with 300 ml/½ pint cream
450 g/1 lb fresh strawberries

Combine the ground almonds and sugar in a bowl. Sift the flour with the salt on to a flat work surface and add the ground almond mixture. Pound the butter with a rolling pin to soften. Make a large well in the centre of the flour mixture and add the softened butter and egg yolk. Using your fingertips, quickly work the centre ingredients until partly mixed. Gradually work in the flour mixture to form coarse crumbs. Lightly flour the work surface and knead the dough lightly. The dough should be smooth and pliable. Press the dough into a ball, wrap in greaseproof paper or cling film and chill it for 30 minutes.

Grease 3 baking sheets and preheat the oven to moderately hot (190 C, 375 F, gas 5). Divide the dough into 3 equal portions. With the heel of your hand, press each portion into a 23-cm/8-in round on a prepared baking sheet. If available, place flan rings around the edge to keep the dough from spreading. Bake for 10 to 12 minutes until golden brown. If not using flan rings, trim the rounds while still warm, using a plate or lid as a guide. Cut one round into 6 to 8 uniform wedges. Transfer the wedges and the whole rounds to a rack to cool.

Not more than 2 hours before serving, prepare the Chantilly Cream. Set aside about a third for decoration and put it in a piping bag fitted with a medium star nozzle. Hull and halve the strawberries, reserving 7 or 9 whole strawberries for decoration. Place one round of pastry on a platter, spread with cream and top with half the cut strawberries. Cover with more chantilly cream. Place the second round of pastry on top and spread with chantilly cream. Using piping bag, pipe 6 to 8 lines of chantilly cream from centre to edge of round, marking 6 to 8 equal sections. Arrange the remaining cut strawberries between the lines of chantilly cream. Top each section with a wedge of pastry placed at a 45° angle and supported by a line of chantilly cream. Pipe a rosette of chantilly cream on each wedge and one in the centre of the torte. Place a strawberry in the centre of each rosette. **Serves 6–8**

Caramelised Apple Pie

Tarte Tatin

Named after two impoverished sisters who had to earn their living by baking their father's favourite pie.

1 quantity sweet flan pastry (page 112)
1 kg/2 lb Golden Delicious apples
juice of 1 lemon
1 cup water

Chill the pastry for at least 30 minutes. Peel, halve and core the apples, then rub with lemon juice to prevent discoloration. Preheat oven to moderately hot (190 C, 375 F, gas 5). In a heavy saucepan, gently heat the sugar and water until the sugar dissolves, then boil to a golden brown caramel. Remove from the heat and let the bubbles subside, then pour the hot caramel into a 20-cm/8-in heavy frying pan with a metal handle or a heavy ovenproof dish, turning it to coat the bottom evenly with caramel. Pack the apple halves upright and overlapping in circles on the caramel to cover it completely. Bake uncovered on the bottom shelf of the oven for 20 minutes, then cool slightly, allowing steam to evaporate.

Roll out the chilled pastry dough to a 23-cm/9-in circle, 5 mm/¼ in thick, and chill on a baking sheet for 15 minutes or until firm. Place the pastry circle on the apples to cover completely, tucking in the edges. Prick the dough several times with a fork. Bake for 20 minutes or until the crust is light golden. If the apples are not tender, cook a little longer. Cool the pie to lukewarm in the frying pan or baking dish, then place a warmed serving plate over the top and invert together. Remove the frying pan or baking dish. If any apples stick to the bottom, remove with a spatula and replace on the pie. Serve warm or at room temperature. **Serves 6**

Fruit Tartlets

Tartelettes aux Fruits

Few desserts are as tempting as a display of fresh fruit tartlets – be sure to choose contrasting colours.

1 quantity sweet flan pastry (page 117)
apricot jam glaze (page 111) *or* redcurrant jelly glaze (see below)
selection of fresh fruit such as strawberries, raspberries, black or green grapes, cherries and tangerines
REDCURRANT JELLY GLAZE
350-g/12-oz jar redcurrant jelly
2 teaspoons water

Chill the sweet flan pastry for at least 30 minutes. Grease eight 8-cm/3½-in tartlet moulds. Roll out the chilled dough 5 mm/¼ in thick and use to line the moulds. Chill until the dough is firm.

Heat the oven to moderately hot (190 C, 375 F, gas 5) and bake the tartlets blind for 10–15 minutes. Allow to cool. Prepare the jam or jelly glaze. Prepare the chosen fruit: hull the strawberries, halving large ones, pick over the raspberries, stone the grapes or cherries, and peel and segment the tangerines. Brush the tartlet shells with melted jam or jelly glaze to help prevent the fruit juice from making the pastry soggy. Arrange the fruit in the shells in an attractive pattern and brush generously with glaze. Red fruit should be coated with redcurrant jelly glaze and green and yellow fruits with apricot jam glaze. Serve the filled tartlets at room temperature within 6 to 8 hours. **Makes 8**

Redcurrant Jelly Glaze

In a small non-aluminium saucepan, melt the redcurrant jelly with 1 tablespoon water. Stir gently but do not whisk or the jelly will become cloudy. Do not cook more than 1 to 2 minutes after melting or the jelly will darken. Extra glaze can be stored in an airtight container. Reheat to melt before using.

Puff Pastry

Far left Fold each corner of the rolled-out dough over the softened square of butter.

Centre Bubbles in the dough indicate the presence of air between layers of butter and dough. This will help the pastry rise.

Left Fold the rectangle of dough into three. This process of rolling out and folding is called a *turn*.

Puff Pastry

Pâte Feuilletée

Place a baking tray full of ice on your work surface to cool it.

200 to 225 g/ 7 to 8 oz	**unsalted butter**	300 to 375 g/ 11 to 13 oz
225 g/8 oz	**plain flour**	375 g/13 oz
1 teaspoon	**salt**	$1\frac{1}{2}$ teaspoons
1 teaspoon	**lemon juice**	$1\frac{1}{2}$ teaspoons
6–8 tablespoons	**cold water**	175 to 200 ml/ 6 to 7 fl oz

Melt 15 g/$\frac{1}{2}$ oz of the butter and chill the remainder. Sift the flour on to a marble slab or your cooled work surface and make a well in the centre. Place the salt, lemon juice, smaller quantity of water and the melted butter in the well and mix these ingredients briefly with your fingertips. Gradually work in the flour, using the fingertips of both hands until the mixture resembles coarse crumbs. If the mixture is dry add a little more water, a few drops at a time. Cut the dough several times to ensure that the ingredients are thoroughly mixed, but do not knead. Press the dough into a ball, wrap and chill for 15 minutes.

Lightly flour the butter and soften by pounding with a rolling pin. When flattened, fold it in half and continue to fold and flatten until the butter is pliable but not sticky. The butter should be as close as possible to the dough in consistency. Shape the butter into a 15-cm/6-in square. Roll out the dough to a 30-cm/12-in square so it is slightly thicker in the centre than at the sides. Set the butter in the centre of the dough and fold the dough around it like an envelope. Place this parcel, seams side down, on the work surface and press the rolling pin on to it a few times to flatten it slightly.

Roll the dough out to a rectangle about 18 to 20 cm/7 to 8 in wide and 45 to 50 cm/18 to 20 in long. Fold one end of the rectangle over the other so it looks like a neatly folded business letter. Gently press the seams with a rolling pin to seal and turn the dough a quarter turn to bring the seam side to your left. This is called a 'turn'. Repeat the rolling and folding process to complete a second turn. Wrap the dough and chill for 15 minutes. Repeat again to give the dough 4 turns. Chill for another 15 minutes, then repeat the rolling and folding process, giving 6 turns in all. The dough can be refrigerated overnight after the fourth turn. Chill the dough for at least an hour before using.

Apple Turnovers

Chaussons aux Pommes

(Illustrated on back endpaper)
'Chaussons' literally means 'woolly socks' – an inelegant but vivid name for these warming apple turnovers.

puff pastry (page 115) made with 200 to 225 g/7 to 8 oz butter
40 g/1½ oz butter
675 g/1½ lb Golden Delicious apples, peeled, cored and sliced
2 to 3 tablespoons caster sugar
beaten egg to glaze
25 g/1 oz icing sugar

Prepare the puff pastry, completing all six turns. Chill for at least 1 hour. Heat the butter in a large frying pan. Add the apples and sprinkle with the sugar. Cook quickly over medium heat, shaking the pan occasionally, until the apple slices are transparent and lightly caramelised. Cool the apples, then chill.

Preheat the oven to hot (220 C, 425 F, gas 7). Sprinkle a baking sheet with water. Roll out the chilled dough 5 mm/¼ in thick. Stamp out 10-cm/4-in rounds with a fluted biscuit cutter. Put a spoonful of cold cooked apples in the centre of each round; do not overfill or the turnovers will burst. Brush the borders with beaten egg and fold the rounds over to make half circles. Press the edges with a fork to seal. Transfer the pastries to a baking sheet and brush the tops with beaten egg. Make 3 slits in the top of each with a knife point to let steam escape. Chill for 10 to 15 minutes then bake for 20 to 25 minutes until risen and browned. Remove from the oven.

Heat the grill. Sprinkle the tops with icing sugar and grill for a few seconds to obtain a shiny glaze, being careful not to burn the sugar. Serve hot or cold. Apple Turnovers are best eaten the day they are baked. **Makes 20**

Palm Leaves

Palmiers

These pastries are golden with caramel which is formed when sugar in the dough browns in the oven.

puff pastry (page 115) made with 200 to 225 g/7 to 8 oz butter *or* 450 g/1 lb puff pastry trimmings
about 225 g/8 oz sugar

Prepare the puff pastry, completing four turns, then chill for at least 1 hour. Make the last two turns, sprinkling the work surface with sugar instead of flour. If using puff pastry trimmings, give two extra turns, using sugar instead of flour on the work surface. Chill the dough for at least 30 minutes. Sprinkle two baking sheets with water. Preheat the oven to hot (220 C, 425 F, gas 7). Roll out the dough to a 50 × 30 cm/20 × 12 in) rectangle, continuing to use sugar on the work surface. Trim the edges. Fold one long edge over twice to reach the centre of the dough. Repeat with the other long edge. Press the folded dough lightly with a rolling pin to seal. Fold one folded section of the dough on top of the other and press lightly with a rolling pin. Use a sharp knife to cut the dough into 5-mm/¼-in slices.

Place on the prepared baking sheets, leaving room to let the 'leaves' more than double in size. Open the slices slightly to round them. Chill for 15 minutes. Bake 6 to 8 minutes until the undersides begin to brown. Turn the leaves over with a metal spatula and bake for a further 3 to 4 minutes longer until golden. These burn quickly, so watch carefully. **Makes about 30**

Cream Slice

Mille Feuille

The French name for this flaky layered dessert means a thousand leaves.

puff pastry (page 115) made with 200 to 225 g/7 to 8 oz butter
2 to 3 tablespoons apricot jam glaze (page 111)
Chantilly Cream (page 117) made with 150 ml/¼ pint cream
3 tablespoons raspberry jam
Icing
100 g/4 oz icing sugar
1 tablespoon kirsch, rum or liqueur
1 tablespoon water

Prepare the puff pastry, completing all six turns, and chill for at least 1 hour. Preheat the oven to hot (220 C, 425 F, gas 7). Roll out the dough as thin as possible to a rectangle large enough to cover a 25 × 35-cm/10 × 14-in baking sheet. Sprinkle water over the baking sheet and place the pastry on top. Prick the pastry several times with a fork. Chill for 10 to 15 minutes, then bake for 10 minutes or until golden. Reduce the oven temperature to moderate (180 C, 350 F, gas 4) and bake for a further 5 minutes. Loosen the pastry with a metal spatula, turn it over and bake for a further 5 minutes or until very crisp. Transfer to a rack to cool.

Not more than 3 hours before serving, trim the edges of the rectangle. Crush the trimmings and reserve. Cut the pastry rectangle lengthwise into three equal strips. Brush the top layer with apricot jam glaze and leave to stand. The glaze prevents the icing making the pastry soggy.

Prepare the icing. Sift the icing sugar into a bowl. Beat in the kirsch, rum or liqueur and a little of the water. Mix to a smooth stiff paste. Place the bowl in a pan of hot water and heat the icing to lukewarm; the icing should be thick enough to coat the back of a spoon. If too thick, add more water. If too thin, beat in more sifted icing sugar. While still warm spread this over the top layer.

Prepare the Chantilly Cream. Spread one strip of pastry with raspberry jam, top with another strip and spread that also with Chantilly Cream. Set the iced strip of pastry on top and press lightly. Press the reserved pastry crumbs around the sides. Chill thoroughly. Just before serving, cut into 4 to 5-cm/1½ to 2-in slices with a serrated knife. **Serves 8**

Chantilly Cream

Crème Chantilly

150 ml/¼ pint few drops 1 teaspoon	**double or whipping cream vanilla essence icing sugar**	300 ml/½ pint few drops 1½ teaspoons
450 ml/¾ pint ¼ teaspoon 2 teaspoons	**double or whipping cream vanilla essence icing sugar**	600 ml/1 pint ½ teaspoon 1 tablespoon

Chill the cream, bowl and whisk before starting. Using a balloon whisk or electric beater whip the cream until it starts to thicken. Add the vanilla essence and sugar. Continue beating until the cream holds its shape and sticks to the whisk or beaters. Be careful not to overbeat or the cream will separate.

Choux Pastry

Pâte à Choux

50 g/2 oz	**plain flour**	100 g/4 oz
125 ml/4 fl oz	**water**	250 ml/8 fl oz
¼ teaspoon	**salt**	¾ teaspoon
50 g/2 oz	**butter**	100 g/4 oz
2	**eggs**	4

Sift the flour on to a piece of greaseproof paper. In a saucepan heat the water, salt and butter until the butter is melted. Bring just to the boil and add all the flour at once. Beat vigorously with a wooden spoon until the mixture is smooth and pulls away from the sides of the pan to form a ball. Beat for 30 seconds to 1 minute over very low heat to dry the mixture. Remove from the heat and allow to cool slightly.

Beat the eggs together, then add a little at a time to the dough, beating thoroughly after each addition. Continue until the dough is very shiny and just falls from the spoon. It is important to obtain the correct consistency; all the egg may not be needed. If not using immediately, rub the surface of the dough with butter to prevent a skin forming.

Chocolate Eclairs

Éclairs au Chocolat

choux pastry (page 117) made with 100 g/4 oz flour
beaten egg to glaze
CHOCOLATE CREAM FILLING
75 g/3 oz plain chocolate, coarsely chopped
450 ml/$\frac{3}{4}$ pint milk
6 egg yolks
100 g/4 oz sugar
50 g/2 oz plain flour
CHOCOLATE ICING
200 g/7 oz icing sugar
25 g/1 oz plain chocolate, coarsely chopped
$\frac{1}{2}$ to 3 tablespoons water

Preheat the oven to moderately hot (200 C, 400 F, gas 6). Lightly grease two baking sheets. Spoon the choux pastry into a piping bag fitted with a 1-cm/$\frac{1}{2}$-in plain nozzle. Pipe 10-cm/4-in strips of dough on to the prepared baking sheets, leaving enough room for the éclairs to double in size. Brush with beaten egg, smoothing the surface at the same time. Bake for 25 to 30 minutes until firm and browned. Transfer the éclairs to a rack to cool.

Meanwhile prepare the chocolate cream filling. Melt the chocolate in a bowl over a pan of hot water, then allow to cool slightly. Scald the milk by bringing it just to the boil. Beat the egg yolks with the sugar until pale and creamy, then stir in the flour. Whisk in half the hot milk then whisk the mixture back into the remaining hot milk in a saucepan. Bring just to the boil, whisking constantly. Remove from the heat and cool to lukewarm before beating in the melted chocolate. If not using immediately, rub the surface with butter to prevent a skin forming.

Next make the chocolate icing. Sift the icing sugar into a bowl. Melt the chocolate in a bowl over a pan of boiling water and beat this with $\frac{1}{2}$ to 1 tablespoon water into the icing sugar. Mix to a smooth, stiff paste. Place the bowl in a pan of hot water and heat to lukewarm. The icing should be thick enough to coat the back of a spoon. If too thick add a little more water. If too thin beat in more sifted icing sugar. Use while still warm.

Dip the top of each éclair in the icing and leave to stand in a dry place. Not more than two hours before serving spoon the chocolate cream filling into a piping bag fitted with a 5-mm/$\frac{1}{4}$-in plain nozzle. Poke two holes in the side of each éclair with the tip of the tube and pipe the filling into each hole to fill the éclair. **Makes 16 to 20**

Cream Puffs

Choux à la Crème

(Illustrated on back endpaper)
Try to pipe the puffs so all are the same size to ensure even baking.

choux pastry (page 117) made with 100 g/4 oz flour
beaten egg to glaze
Chantilly Cream (page 117) made with 300 ml/$\frac{1}{2}$ pint cream
25 g/1 oz icing sugar

Preheat the oven to moderately hot (200 C, 400 F, gas 6). Lightly grease two baking sheets. Spoon the pastry into a piping bag fitted with a 1-cm/$\frac{1}{2}$-in plain nozzle. Pipe 4-cm/1$\frac{1}{2}$-in mounds of pastry on the prepared baking sheets. Alternatively drop mounds of dough on to the baking sheet using two spoons. Leave room between the puffs to let them double in size. Brush with beaten egg, smoothing the surface at the same time. Bake for 25 to 30 minutes until firm and browned. Transfer the puffs to a rack to cool.

Not more than two hours before serving, prepare the Chantilly cream. Spoon the cream into a piping bag fitted with a 5-mm/$\frac{1}{4}$-in plain nozzle. Cut a slit in each puff just large enough to insert the nozzle. Fill the puffs with cream. Sprinkle with icing sugar and arrange on a serving plate. **Makes 20**

Chantilly Swans

Choux pastry is the right consistency for piping when it falls thickly from the spoon.

Pipe Chantilly Cream into the baked swan bodies. Arrange necks and wings in the cream and sprinkle with icing sugar.

Chantilly Swans

Cygnes Chantilly

These graceful swans are almost too pretty to eat.

choux pastry (page 117) made with 100 g/4 oz flour
beaten egg to glaze
Chantilly Cream (page 117) made with 300 ml/$\frac{1}{2}$ pint cream
25 g/1 oz icing sugar

Preheat the oven to moderately hot (200 C, 400 F, gas 6). Lightly grease two baking sheets. Spoon the choux pastry into a bag fitted with a 9-mm/$\frac{3}{8}$-in plain nozzle. Pipe ten to twelve ovals about 4 × 8-cm/1$\frac{1}{2}$ × 3-in on one baking sheet for the swan's bodies, leaving enough room for them to double in size. Hold a 5-mm/$\frac{1}{4}$-in plain nozzle firmly over the 9-mm/$\frac{3}{8}$-in one and pipe fifteen S-shapes about 8 to 10-cm/3 to 4-in long on the second sheet. The few extra are to allow for breakage. Brush the bodies and necks with beaten egg, smoothing the surface at the same time. Bake the necks for 10 to 15 minutes until firm and browned. Bake the bodies for a further 10–15 minutes until also crisp and browned. Transfer to a rack to cool.

Not more than 2 hours before serving prepare the Chantilly Cream. Spoon it into a piping bag fitted with a 9-mm/$\frac{3}{8}$-in star nozzle. Cut the oval puffs in half horizontally then cut each top piece in half lengthwise for the wings. Pipe in enough cream to fill the bottom half of each body. Insert the neck at one end of the body and place the wings in the cream at an angle so they spread up and out from the neck (see illustration). Sprinkle with icing sugar and arrange on a serving dish. **Makes 10–12**

Strawberry Savarin

Savarin aux Fraises

The dough for savarin and babas is very similar, but savarin is always baked in a ring.

225 g/8 oz strawberries
3 tablespoons caster sugar
175 g/6 oz plain flour
2 tablespoons warm water
15 g/½ oz fresh yeast or 1½ teaspoons dried yeast
3 eggs
generous pinch salt
50 g/2 oz butter, softened
1–2 tablespoons rum
3 tablespoons redcurrant jelly
SYRUP
200 g/7 oz granulated sugar
300 ml/½ pint water
thinly pared rind and juice of ½ lemon

Hull the strawberries and sprinkle with 1 tablespoon of the sugar. Cover and refrigerate for 1 to 2 hours. Sift the flour into a large warmed bowl. Make a well in the centre of the flour and sprinkle over the dried yeast. If using fresh yeast, cream it with a little of the lukewarm water then add it to the rest in the well. Leave for 5 minutes.

Add the eggs, salt and the remaining 2 tablespoons sugar and combine these with the yeast and water. Gradually draw in the flour to make a smooth dough. Beat vigorously with cupped fingers, raising the mixture and allowing it to fall back into the bowl with a slap. Continue beating for 5 minutes until the dough is smooth and elastic. Alternatively use an electric mixer fitted with a dough hook and beat until smooth and elastic. Cover the bowl with a clean, damp tea-towel and leave in a warm place for 45 minutes to 1 hour or until the dough is doubled in size.

Grease a 1.15-litre/2-pint savarin or ring mould. Beat the softened butter into the prepared mould and cover again with the damp tea-towel. Leave in a warm place for 45 minutes to 1 hour or until the dough rises to the top of the mould. Preheat the oven to moderately hot (200 C, 400 F, gas 6). Bake for 20 to 25 minutes until the savarin is browned and shrinks from the side of the mould. Remove from the mould and place on a rack over a tray.

Not more than 4 hours before serving prepare the lemon syrup. Heat the sugar and water together over gentle heat until the sugar is completely dissolved. Add the pared lemon rind and bring to the boil. Simmer for five minutes then remove from the heat, discard the lemon rind and stir in the lemon juice. Spoon the hot syrup over the savarin, allowing it to absorb as much as possible. The savarin should swell and look shiny.

Transfer the savarin to a serving plate. Just before serving sprinkle over the rum and pile the strawberries in the centre of the ring. Melt the jelly in a small saucepan and brush over the strawberries and savarin to glaze. **Serves 4–6**

Rum Babas

Babas au Rhum

(Illustrated on back endpaper)
Dariole moulds are traditionally used for making babas but any small deep ovenproof mould can be used.

75 g/3 oz currants
4 tablespoons rum
225 g/8 oz plain flour
3 tablespoons warm water
15 g/½ oz fresh yeast or 1½ teaspoons dried yeast
3 eggs
½ teaspoon salt
2 teaspoons sugar
125 g/4½ oz butter, softened
SYRUP
300 g/11 oz sugar
900 ml/1½ pints water

Soak the currants in 3 tablespoons of the rum. Sift the flour into a large warmed bowl. Make a well in the centre and pour in the water. Sprinkle over the yeast. If using fresh yeast, cream it with a little of the water then add to the remaining liquid in the well. Leave to stand for 5 minutes.

Add the eggs, salt and remaining 2 tablespoons sugar and combine these with the yeast and water. Gradually draw in the flour to make a smooth dough. Beat vigorously with cupped fingers, raising the mixture and allowing it to fall back into the bowl with a slap. Continue beating for 5 minutes until the dough is smooth and elastic. Alternatively use an electric mixer fitted with a dough hook and mix until the dough is smooth and elastic. Cover the bowl with a damp tea-towel and leave in a warm place for 45 minutes to 1 hour or until the dough has doubled in size.

Butter twelve dariole moulds. Chill the moulds in the freezer then butter them again. Beat the softened butter into the risen dough until smooth. Drain the currants reserving the rum and stir them into the dough. Drop the dough from a spoon to fill the moulds one-third full. Place them on a baking sheet and cover with a clean damp tea-towel. Leave to rise in a warm place for 45 minutes to 1 hour until the moulds are almost full.

Preheat the oven to moderately hot (200 C, 400 F, gas 6). Bake for 20 to 25 minutes until the babas are browned and begin to shrink from the sides of the moulds. Immediately remove them from the moulds.

Not more than 4 hours ahead prepare the sugar syrup. Heat the sugar with the water over a low heat until the sugar is dissolved. Boil for 2 to 3 minutes until the syrup is clear. Remove from the heat and place the babas in the warm syrup. Carefully turn them several times with a large spoon so they absorb as much syrup as possible. The babas will swell and look shiny. Using a large slotted spoon carefully remove the babas and place on a serving plate. Reserve the remaining syrup. Just before serving sprinkle a little of the rum drained from the currants over the babas. Add the remaining rum to the reserved syrup and serve separately. **Makes 12**

Brioche

Brioche

This rich bread is perfect with morning coffee or tea.

2 tablespoons lukewarm water
15 g/½ oz dried yeast *or* 25 g/1 oz fresh yeast, crumbled
500 g/1 lb 2 oz flour
6 eggs, beaten
2 teaspoons salt
25 g/1 oz sugar
250 g/9 oz unsalted butter
beaten egg to glaze

Put the lukewarm water into a medium bowl, stir in the yeast, then add a little of the flour. Set aside for 5 to 10 minutes until spongy. Sift the remaining flour into the bowl of a large mixer or follow the classic method (below). Add all but about ½ an egg, the salt and sugar to the yeast mixture and mix lightly. Pour the egg and yeast mixture into the flour. Using a mixer fitted with a dough hook, beat the mixture to a soft sticky dough. If the dough is dry, beat in the remaining egg little by little. Pound the butter with your fist or a rolling pin to soften. Beat the butter into the dough, using the dough hook, until completely mixed in. Place the dough in a lightly oiled bowl, turning it to oil all sides. Cover with a clean damp tea-towel and leave to rise at room temperature for 2 hours or until nearly doubled in size.

Place the risen dough on a floured work surface. Fold a third of the dough over the middle third and the remaining third over all, patting to knock out the air. Return to the bowl and cover again with a damp tea-towel. Leave to rise at room temperature until doubled in bulk or overnight in the refrigerator. Brioche dough is much easier to handle if refrigerated.

Grease fifteen 8-cm/3-in brioche moulds or two 16-cm/6-in brioche moulds. Knead the dough gently just to knock out air and divide it into 15 pieces for individual brioches or half for large brioches. Pinch off a third of each piece of dough and shape both large and small pieces into balls. Place a large ball in each brioche pan. Cut a deep cross on top and crown it with the smaller ball of dough. An alternative method is to make holes in the larger balls and place the smaller balls in the holes. Preheat the oven to hot (220 C, 425 F, gas 7). Let the small brioches rise in a warm place for 15 minutes and large brioches for 20 to 25 minutes until the moulds are almost full. Brush the risen dough with beaten egg and bake the small brioches for 15 to 20 minutes until browned. Baked brioches will sound hollow when tapped on the bottom. Bake large brioches for 15 minutes, then reduce the oven temperature to moderately hot (190 C, 375 F, gas 5) and bake for a further 30 to 40 minutes until the brioches begin to pull away from the sides of the pans and sound hollow when tapped. Turn out onto a rack to cool. **Makes 15 small or 2 large brioches**

Classic Method for Preparing Brioche Dough

Sift the flour onto a marble slab or board and make a large well in the centre. Place the salt and sugar in piles on one side of the well and the yeast on the other side. Combine the yeast with the warm water, in the well, being careful not to mix in any salt or sugar at this stage. Leave for 5 to 10 minutes or until spongy.

Add all but ½ an egg, the salt and sugar, mixing them together with the fingertips of one hand. Sprinkle with flour, then quickly work the flour into the liquid ingredients to form coarse crumbs. Do not let any liquid escape from the well. If the dough is dry add the remaining egg a little at a time. Press the dough firmly together – it should be soft and sticky – and knead by lifting it up and slapping it down on a floured work surface for 5 to 10 minutes until smooth and elastic. Soften the butter by pounding with a rolling pin then knead it into the dough as lightly as possible until just mixed. Place the dough in a lightly oiled bowl and proceed as recipe above.

Index

Overleaf, at the back Apple Turnovers (page 116); *left*, Lemon Pie (page 112); *right, above*, Cream Puffs (page 118); *right*, Rum Babas (page 120).